Who Am I in Christ?

Jerri Mason

A Study for New Believers

Fulton, KY

Who Am I in Christ?

Copyright © 2019 by Jerri Mason

All rights reserved. No part of this publication may be reproduced, stored in a retrieval system or transmitted in any way by any means, electronic, mechanical, photocopy, recording or otherwise without the prior permission of the author except as provided by USA copyright law.

Scripture quotations taken from the THE HOLY BIBLE, NEW INTERNATIONAL VERSION®, NIV® Copyright © 1973, 1978, 1984, 2011 by Biblica, Inc.™ Used by permission. All rights reserved worldwide.

Published by Master Design Publishing
  an imprint of Master Design Marketing, LLC
  789 State Route 94 E, Fulton, KY 42041
  www.MasterDesign.org

ISBN   Paperback: 978-1-941512-40-1
           Ebook: 978-1-941512-41-8

Cover design and illustrations by Kelley Norcross.

Printed in the USA.

Publisher's Cataloging-In-Publication Data
(Prepared by The Donohue Group, Inc.)

Names: Mason, Jerri, author.
Title: Who am I in Christ? : a study for new believers / Jerri Mason.
Description: Fulton, KY : Master Design Publishing, [2019]
Identifiers: ISBN 9781941512401 | ISBN 9781941512418 (ebook)
Subjects: LCSH: Christian life--Problems, exercises, etc. | Identity (Psychology)--Religious aspects--Christianity--Problems, exercises, etc. | Jesus Christ--Biblical teaching. | Jesus Christ--Knowableness--Problems, exercises, etc. | God (Christianity)--Knowableness--Problems, exercises, etc.
Classification: LCC BV4501.3 .M37 2019 (print) | LCC BV4501.3 (ebook) | DDC 248.4--dc23

Dedication

This book is dedicated to all the
teachers who taught me
God's Word, including my parents,
Lymon and Louise Houston

Contents

Foreword	vi
Preface	vii
Special Thanks	viii
Part 1	1
1. Thy Word is Truth	3
2. My New Life in Christ	9
3. Knowing Whose I Am	19
4. Understanding His Love	27
5. How Do I Talk to You?	33
6. Experiencing His Pressence	41
7. My Blueprint For Life	51
8. How Can I Hear Your Voice?	61
Leaders' Helps	67
Part 2	83
1. Practicing Forgiveness	85
2. Emotions in Motion	91
3. God's Masterpiece	99
4. What Did You Say?	105
5. Redeeming My Time	111
6. Struggles Within	117
7. Pursuing Godliness	123
8. Pass It On	131
Leaders' Helps	139
About the Author	153

Foreword

"It was my joy to be Jerri Mason's pastor for several years. There is no doubt she has a heart for new believers. Her heart is expressed in the work, "Who Am I in Christ?" As you work through Jerri's book you will gain knowledge and understand what it means to grow in the Lord. This is a good opportunity for all Christ-followers to develop good discipleship habits. You will be glad you took the time to use this material as you begin your walk with Christ."

Dr. Ted Kersh
President/Bible Teacher
Author of *Equipped By His Word*

Preface

The Purpose of This Study

I pray also that the eyes of your heart may be enlightened, in order that you may know the Hope to which He has called you, the riches of His glorious inheritance in the saints and His incomparably great power to us who believe.
Ephesians 1:18-19a

My original purpose in writing this study was to share with my three sons, their families, and the generations to come, what God has taught me. With time, friends and church leaders have encouraged me to make the study available to churches and Bible study classes. The study has grown into a study for both men and women. It's for anyone who desires to know who they are in Christ and for those who are looking for a "tool" to share with others. You will need a study Bible and a notebook to record what you learn.

Remember: God's Word is Truth! As you search the Scriptures, Jesus will be the Teacher!

May you be Blessed!

Jerri Mason

Special Thanks

How blessed I was to be brought up in a Christian home in Northwest Arkansas. My parents nurtured me in the Scriptures and encouraged me to walk with God. One of my earliest memory of church is of my mother, Louise Houston, telling Bible stories in the Beginner Sunday School class.

As a young adult it was a privilege to witness firsthand the growth of one of the largest churches in America. This amazing church is still growing today. Because we have lived in several states we have been privileged to be part of many great churches. The following men of God have been my pastors at different times. They have given me insights into the Scriptures for which I will be forever grateful: Rev. Cliff Palmer, Dr. Bailey Smith, Dr. Tom Elliff, Dr. Ronny Floyd, Dr. Rick Reaves, Dr. Jim Burkett, and Dr. Ted Kersh. They have been faithful to proclaim the truths of God's Word and have therefore contributed indirectly to this study.

In addition to these men of God, I have been mentored by Andy and Joan Horner of Premier Designs, Inc. of Dallas, Texas, with whom I have been associated since 1990. Joan went to be with the Lord in 2010.

I am grateful to all of these who have mentored and shaped me. This study is a result of their investment in me.

Part 1

My Relationship with God

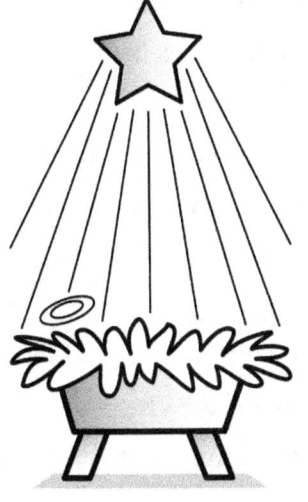

*For God did not send
His Son into the world
to condemn the world,
but to save the world
through Him.
John 3:17 (NIV)*

1. Thy Word is Truth

Where can I find the truth?

God, can I really know you?

Many of us have questions like these. Some questions are more trivial, (like, what was Noah's wife's name?) but we have some serious ones, and they trouble us often. We think about what will happen when we die. We think about God and wonder what to believe. We sometimes doubt what we have been taught and don't know where to get answers to our questions. We see people hurting and we see suffering around us. We ask "why"?

These are questions that most of us at some point in our life have asked and countless books have attempted to answer. Where can we go to really get answers to these and other important questions?

Many of us were taught as children about God and we have grown up accepting what our family and church have taught us. Sometimes friends, teachers, and professors have influenced us and caused us to question what we were taught. We may have read what famous philosophers have written, and often we are confused even more.

Some of us may have not been taught about God at all. Maybe as a child we never heard God's name used in a prayer but only as a curse. Our family may have been broken by unfaithful relationships and/or divorce. Abuse may have been a way of life. The concept of a loving Father may be foreign to us. So, if you have trouble thinking of God as a Heavenly Father or you are confused about what to believe, this study is for you.

It's also for you if you have assurance that you know Christ, and that you have joy in your daily walk with him. We will open God's Word and discover truths that many believers miss. We will find out what it means to be God's child with all the privileges that includes.

So, where do we start? Where do you go to get the truth about God? How can you pass on to your children how to know God and find a real purpose to life? Where can we learn how to be a godly man or woman? The Bible, God's inspired Word is where we find answers and the principles we need to follow throughout life.

The Bible, from beginning to end points us to Jesus Christ. No event in history has affected our world to the extent that the death of Christ has affected us. The Bible is His story. Not only does it provide a way for us to know God and be forgiven of our sins but His life and death affected time itself.

No matter what you believe or who you are, your life operates in time. Units of time, days, months, and years are recorded on a calendar. The calendar is used to schedule appointments and our daily activities. At the center of time is the Cross. In other words, the current year is determined by the life and death of Jesus Christ. The agnostic, the atheist, the believer, all schedule their day based on what happened some 2000 years ago on a hillside outside Jerusalem. God reached out to mankind when He came to earth as a baby in Bethlehem. No One has influenced the world as much as this one solitary life. Jesus Christ turned time around!

"Men spoke from God as they were carried along by the Holy Spirit." Scripture, the Bible, originated with God and has been passed to us! This is how the Bible came to us according to 2 Peter 1:21. If it truly is God's Word to us, why would we neglect it and ignore its instruction? If we want direction in our life, and we need to know what to do, we will find answers in His Word. John 17:7 states "Thy Word is Truth."

Psalm 119:11 says: "Thy Word is a lamp to my feet, and a light unto my path." God has also promised to direct our path in Proverbs 3:5-6. Write it down for later reference in a notebook.

Suggestion: Begin a study notebook with a section of "Bible Promises". Write these two Scriptures there. You will want to add additional truths and Scriptures regularly. If you like the computer, you may want to begin storing the treasures you uncover there. Wherever you choose to begin, plan to be consistent.

The Bible sheds light on countless subjects which have been hidden for a time. These hidden truths are called mysteries. No mystery is as important as the mystery of how we, as sinners, imperfect, finite humans, limited in our understanding, can KNOW the one, true, infinite God in a personal way. God wants each of us to know Him intimately. He always takes the initiative. He reaches out in unconditional love to each of us. He's reaching out to you today.

Will you be open to His voice through His Word?

As was stated earlier, most of us have heard about God all our lives. We have at least some concept of Him. We've heard that God created the world. We've heard of the Garden of Eden and the Devil. We've heard about Noah and the Ark. We may have heard about Jonah and the "whale." We've heard that Jesus died on the cross. Some of us, though, have never personally studied about Him, we only have a vague knowledge of Him.

Remember history class? That's where we all studied facts about famous men and women. Facts about God are obviously more important! The Bible is where we discover for ourselves who God is and how we can know Him in a personal way. So, it's important to open the Bible and look for the Truth that's inside.

(If you are in a class study and you can't afford a Bible, please let the leader of your class know. You will need your own copy to complete these lessons.)

The Bible is God's love letter to you and in time your copy of it will become a treasure. So, consider your choices carefully before you purchase your Bible. It would be wise to ask advice from your pastor or an experienced person at a Christian Bookstore in order to start with a version that you can use for many years. It will become invaluable to you as you grow in your knowledge of God's Word. If possible, choose a leather binding for durability.

1. Thy Word is Truth

In our minds now, let's go back to history class again. Consider these questions: What facts do you know about George Washington? Do you know him or just know about him? What about your family? What do you know about your great grandparents? Do you really KNOW your great grandfather or have you only heard about him through others? What facts have you heard about God? Do you really know Him or just know about Him?

So, are you getting the point, here? Relationship is what we are talking about. Do you have a relationship with God or do you just know "about" Him? If the answer to this last question is – "I'm not sure" or "not really" then, I have good news for you. The Bible tells us that you can know that you know Him, not just know ABOUT Him. You can have a personal relationship with Him. You can experience His love and satisfy the longings of your heart that you may not even realize you have.

When you have a close relationship with someone you are able to communicate easily. You understand that you can "be yourself" and they will trust you and you can trust them. You feel that they care about you and you care about them. What about the way you feel about God? Have you felt lonely at times and wondered if God were even there? Does He really care about you? Can you trust Him? Have you looked up into a starry sky and felt small and insignificant? Have you wondered how all those stars got there and if there is a God, does He know who you are?

Today God will begin to answer your questions if you will open your heart to Him. Your "heart" is the real you! It's the part of you that longs to know God. The Bible says in Jeremiah 29:12, "You will call upon me and come and pray to me, and I will listen to you. You will seek me and find me when you seek me with all your heart."

What needs do you have in your life today?

 *Suggestion: Write this verse and your answers in your notebook under God's Promises*

Only you know why you have started this Bible study. In order for the lessons to be effective, there needs to be a desire in your heart to find what God has for you in His Word. There must be a willingness to open your Bible and actually think about and answer the questions. So, will you seek Him with all your heart today? Will you commit to complete this short study?

What do you hope to learn?

 *Suggestion: 1. Begin a "journal section" in your notebook. Write your goals for this study on today's date. 2. Begin a "Prayer requests" section in your notebook. List your needs or prayer requests in this section.*

Jesus answered, "I am the way and the truth and the life. No one comes to the Father except through me. If you really knew me, you would know my Father as well."
John 14:6

2. My New Life in Christ

Can I Trust You?

Trust - it is so important. When we talk about a relationship there is nothing more important. In our family, in our profession, in our faith – it's crucial to know that we can trust others. We've already discussed how you feel about God. Do you feel you can trust him? Are you honest and transparent with him?

Sometimes it's a challenge for us to examine our feelings and be willing to express them. However, God created us with feelings. It's important for us to face the way we feel about Him. Even though it may make you uncomfortable, your answers to these questions are beneficial in order to understand your relationship with God. (Be assured, there are no right or wrong answers when it comes to expressing feelings and you won't be asked to discuss them with others in the class.)

Has there been a time that you did something wrong and you felt horribly guilty? Did you feel like you had disappointed God or your parents? (Or someone else?) Maybe when you were young you took something that didn't belong to you. Maybe you told a little white lie, or cheated on a test. If you felt ashamed or guilty, that means that your conscience was working. God uses our conscience throughout life to speak to us to make us aware of our sin. Sometimes we may feel like God is near us but the guilt of our sin at other times may cause us to feel like He's not with us at all. As we get older our conscience can become calloused to sin.

Sometimes when we experience difficulties, tragedies, and heartache we pray to God. We can feel His love through others. However, with time, when the pain that we are experiencing fades, so does our closeness to Him. We become aware of that emptiness inside again and we long to experience His love and peace. This confusion may become a continual way of life. So, what part do feelings play in our relationship to God?

Do feelings really matter at all?

Yes, feelings matter a great deal! They are important because they are evidence of what is going on in our heart. Our heart, as referred to in Scripture, involves our mind, our will, and our emotions, or feelings. God speaks to us through our heart. He may use circumstances, even difficulties, to encourage us to turn to Him. It's sometimes easy to blame God for our hardships. However, as we grow in our understanding, we realize that He does not cause pain and suffering. He does use it for good in our life.

Often when we are in the midst of pain and suffering we can't see how God could ever use our circumstance or loss for good. However, with time, we see that good, in fact, was a result.

If you have an example of how God has used tragedy, disappointment, or loss in your life for good, record it in your journal on today's date.

GETTING PAST MY PAST

Spend a few moments thinking about your important relationships. The reason this is helpful is that we can let people who have hurt us be a stumbling block to us and keep us from a relationship with God. We may not realize the impact a certain situation has had on us. Many people let their feelings control them and they find it difficult to ever trust God because someone they looked up to disappointed or offended them.

If this has happened to you, write a summary of the experience in your journal.

Now, let's consider people who are close to you. Write down an example of how your feelings have changed through the years with your family and friends.

Who can you trust completely?

What has enabled you to trust them?

Was there a time that you felt close to God? (If yes, what changed?)

Should we blame God for bad things that happen to us or others? Why or why not?

Broken relationships take time to heal. If trust has been lost, sometimes it takes time for a relationship to be re-established. In fact, it may never happen if we feel we can never trust the one who has offended us. Fortunately, most of us have family and close friends that we trust and we can count on.

When we meet someone we are often guarded. As relationships develop, we begin to understand the way the other thinks, what they like or dislike. We discover their strengths and weaknesses. We learn what and who the other loves. We start to know this person.

So, does my relationship with people affect my relationship to God?

Has someone in the church disappointed you or caused you hurt?

Should we blame God for bad things that happen to us or others?

(In the next unit of study we will discover what God says we must do to restore broken relationships. For now, write down the hurts that you have experienced and ask God to give you His grace to forgive those who have hurt you. Forgiveness is a choice we make. God's grace is

the channel that enables us to forgive. "Feelings" of forgiveness may not always follow our decision to forgive.)

FAITH – What is it?

Without, faith, it is impossible to personally know God. A synonym for FAITH is TRUST. As we have just discussed, trust is extremely important in developing human relationships. If we don't trust a person, we will distance ourselves from him (or her).

FAITH is the element that makes Christianity different from any other religion. It's important to remember here that TRUST is the key to knowing God. If our concept of God is that He's like a "big policeman in the sky" just waiting to zap us if we do something bad, then we will have trouble trusting Him. It's important to understand God's true nature as revealed in Scripture. The more we understand who He is, the more easily we can trust Him. So consider the following:

 How would you describe God?

Which of the following is more important?
   1) What you know about God
   2) How you feel about God
   3) Your faith in God

Which of these words more accurately describes your relationship with God: Trying or trusting?

If you answered trusting, where do you struggle with trusting God?

Do you struggle with trying to please people?

Do you struggle with trying to please God?
Explain your answer if you can.

A THOUGHT TO PONDER:

More than likely, you are sitting at this moment while you are doing this lesson. Your weight is resting on a piece of furniture. What would happen if that chair you are sitting in would fall apart?

Obviously you would fall because you are resting or trusting in that chair to hold you up.

Who or what are you trusting in to go to heaven?

(Record your answer in your journal.)

TIME TO DECIDE:

Knowing Christ personally, having a relationship with Him, begins the moment that you invite Him to come into your life as Savior and Lord. So, what do these words mean?

"Jesus as your Savior" means that you recognize that you have sin in your life, as we all do. Our sin separates us from God and keeps us from a relationship with Him. Jesus, as Savior, left Heaven and came to Earth to pay the debt for our sin. On the cross, He suffered for each of us so we won't have to suffer for our own sin. He paid our sin debt with His blood. When we acknowledge that fact and ask Him to save us from sin, He forgives us of our sins and comes into our hearts. This is a choice we each must make, and it involves an act of our will. Jesus is a gentleman. He knocks at your heart's door (Rev. 3:20) but the doorknob (your will) is on the inside.

"Jesus as Lord" means that we invite Him to be the boss of our life. We give Him our will and we submit to His will for us as He reveals it to us in His Word.

Each of us must open our heart's door to Him and ask Him to come into our life and forgive our sin. Will you trust Him and give Him the "Throne Room" of your heart? Will you, in faith, give Him every part of your life?

Remember, He suffered and died for your sins. When He hung on the cross, all of your sins were placed upon Him, past, present, and future. He knew every sin you would ever commit. (Rom. 5:8) He took your punishment upon Himself. He loves you with a perfect Father's love. He wants to bless you. You can trust Him to come into every area of your life. Will you?

If the answer is "Yes" then simply pray a prayer similar to this.

Let it be your prayer.

"Lord Jesus, I know that I am a sinner. I realize for the first time that I can't go to heaven on my own. I realize that You love me and that You came to earth and died to pay for my sin and to give me eternal life. Come into my life and forgive me of my sin. Take control of every area of my life, be my Savior and Lord. I surrender my life to You. Help me to obey You every day. Thank You for forgiving me and giving me eternal life. In Jesus' name. Amen."

If you sincerely prayed and asked Jesus to come into your life, then WELCOME TO THE FAMILY OF GOD! YOU are now a child of the King! Your inheritance, all of God's riches is yours in Christ Jesus. According to His Word, you have, as a present possession, eternal life and many more wonderful privileges as His child.

(Put this date in your journal as the day you trusted Christ and became His child.)

We want everyone who reads this to be sure that they have a personal relationship with God, through His Son, Jesus. The reason we have done this is because that is the foundation of our faith and it will determine where you will spend eternity.

Now what? This study will give you more insights into the wonderful privileges that you now have as His child. (Read 1 John 3:1) This is truly a new beginning.

> *"Therefore, if anyone is in Christ, he is a new creation; the old has gone, the new has come!" (2 Cor. 5:17 NIV)*

As a new child of God, it's important that you surround yourself with influences that will build you up in the faith. Find a church that teaches God's Word. Not all churches do that. You may want to talk with the pastor or ask for a copy of the church doctrine. Denominations have developed because of the different interpretations of basic beliefs that are taught in the Bible.

Here are some important biblical truths to consider when looking for a church.

Ask if they believe:

1. The Bible is the inspired and inerrent Word of God.
2. God is One God, made of three Persons: God the Father, God the Son, God the Holy Spirit (The Trinity)
3. God (The Trinity) created the Universe.
4. Jesus (God, the Son) was born of a virgin.
5. Jesus lived a sinless life.
6. Jesus died to pay the sin debt of the entire world.
7. Jesus rose again, defeating the devil, and is alive today.
8. Salvation is by grace, through faith, in Christ alone.

9. Jesus will return at the appointed time to gather His church.

10. Jesus will reign forevermore!

In addition to knowing what a church believes and what its main doctrines are, it's also important to sense God's Presence when you attend the services. Some services are informal and have a casual, relaxed atmosphere. Some are friendly but shallow in message. Some use contemporary worship with choruses and a worship band. Others are more formal in atmosphere and may have a choir and orchestra. There are blends of all these types. Some are small congregations. Others are large, with a small church atmosphere. The most important characteristic is, a healthy church will be growing and baptizing new believers. They will often provide classes for new believers as well.

There's usually a difference in the ministries and activities that are offered from one church to another. It may take a while to know for sure which church fits your needs. No matter the size of the church, it's important to attend a small group in order to get acquainted and feel part of the Family.

When you find the right church, the next thing you need to do is find out the requirements to become part of that local church fellowship. Christ gave commands to His Church, each with a specific purpose. One command was for new believers to be baptized as a symbol of their new life in Christ and to identify with Him before men.

Secondly, He commanded that believers observe the Last Supper (sometimes referred to as the Lord's Supper or Communion). New Testament churches regularly practice these two ordinances:

Explain how each one pictures the death and resurrection:

1. Baptism (by Immersion)

2. Lord's Supper (Communion)

When you become a member of a local church you will have a sense of belonging. It will also give you a place to serve God. It will provide you with new friends who have values that will be a positive influence in your life. The day you are baptized is important because it is the day you identify yourself as a follower of Christ and become a member of the local church.

I WAS BAPTIZED ON: (Record the location and date in your journal.)

It will take a while to remember the names of your new "family." So it will be helpful to write their names and contact information in your notebook.

And if the Spirit of Him who raised Jesus from the dead is living in you, He who raised Christ from the dead will also give life to your mortal bodies through His Spirit, who lives in you.
Romans 8:11

3. Knowing Whose I Am

Trying or Trusting?

Christianity though often referred to as a religion, is really not one! Christianity is based on a personal relationship with God. Simply speaking, religion is a belief system which includes rules to live by, which, if obeyed, enables a person to please God. Our relationship with Christ is not based on trying to please Him through our own efforts. If we are pleasing to Him, it's not because of what we have or haven't done, but rather because of what Christ does through us. Our love for Him and desire to please Him is based on *trusting* rather than on *trying*.

As a child of God, getting to know Christ should become a priority. God's Spirit draws us to his Word and to want to be with other believers. It's important that we listen to His nudging in our heart as He leads us.

Jesus is completely God and completely man. Knowing Jesus is how we come to know God the Father. We can't understand that, but the Bible teaches it to be true. Jesus created the universe, became flesh, was born of a virgin, lived a sinless life, died to pay our sin debt, and rose again, thereby overcoming the devil. He ascended into Heaven and is alive today!

Christ said in John 14:6, "I am the Way, and the Truth and the Life. No one comes to the Father except through Me." Also in John 8:19 Jesus said "If you knew me, you would know my Father also." With this statement Jesus claimed to be equal with God the Father. This was very disruptive to the Jews of that day. He went on to state in John 8:58 "I tell you the truth, before Abraham was born. I am". This statement refers to Exodus 3:14. By saying this, Jesus claimed to be the Messiah.

So, with these thought provoking passages before us, let's open God's Word together and learn who Jesus is and who He made us to be.

In addition to the verse just mentioned above, there are several passages in the New Testament that begin with the words "I am". They are extremely important because Jesus spoke them of himself. These metaphors would be good to come back to for a future study. At that point you may want to look up each word in your concordance and do a word study on each one. For now, just write each metaphor and verse in your notebook. If God shows you the significance of these descriptions be sure to include it in your notes.

3. Knowing Whose I Am

"I AM":
John 4:14 – The Water of Life
John 6:35 – The Bread of Life
John 8:12 – The Light of the World
John 10:7 – The Door (or Gate)
John 10:11 – The Shepherd
John 11:25 – The Resurrection and the Life
John 14:6 – The Way, The Truth, and The Life
John 15:5 - The Vine

As His followers observed Jesus daily they grew in understanding of who He was. Notice in the following verses what each person in the passage believed about Christ. Some began to recognize that his teachings were from God. Some called him "Teacher". Some recognized him as a prophet. They continued to listen and they were amazed at what they heard.

KNOWING JESUS AS A GOOD EXAMPLE / TEACHER/PROPHET

Suggestion: Record what you learn from each passage in your journal.)
John 7:40-44
John 20:16-18
John 9:11; 17; 24-25

Many people who heard about Jesus, and listened to Him teach, questioned His authority and they didn't see that His teachings were meant for them. Their spiritual pride blinded them from recognizing their sin and seeing their need of a Savior. They were looking for a Messiah who would deliver them and rule and reign with authority. Jesus, the carpenter from Nazareth just didn't fit their image. Jesus came to "seek and to save" the lost. Why do you think some didn't recognize him?

Think about the following, and write down what it means to you:

We are sinners not because we sin, but we sin because we are sinners.

We all have the tendency to make excuses for sin and blame others. We may deny sin's importance by saying "everyone does it." This blame game goes back all the way to the Garden of Eden. However, there's no excuse for sin. It can't be ignored. Its penalty had to be paid. Since sin entered the world through the sin of Adam (read Romans 5:12), this tendency to sin has passed to us. We can do nothing to remedy the sin problem ourselves. We cannot, therefore, be sure that Heaven will be our home without intervention from God Himself. We cannot live good enough to deserve Heaven. No one can.

The standard for Heaven is perfection. Since we cannot achieve perfection, God provided a way through His Son for us to receive this wonderful gift of salvation from sin. We must come to Jesus and receive this forgiveness of sin and the gift of eternal life.

(If you missed the last lesson please go back and cover the material to affirm your personal relationship with Christ. We can't grow into a relationship with God apart from a spiritual birth into His family.)

KNOWING JESUS AS SAVIOR AND LORD

The New Testament continues to speak of what His followers understood about Jesus. In the following Scriptures, note who is speaking and paraphrase what each one said about Christ.

Why is it important to understand who Jesus is?

John 1:1-2, 10-14

John 3:16-18

John 6:68-69

John 9:35-38

John 20:28

The Holy Spirit comes to live inside us when we trust Christ as our Savior. He is also God, part of the Trinity, and He is the One who enables us to understand the Scriptures, grow in Christ-likeness, and empowers us to live the Christian life. (Please notice, He is a Person and should never be referred to in third person as "it.")

Just as we, on our own, cannot deserve Heaven, neither can we live a life that will please God without His Grace and His Spirit working in and through us.

How do the following Scriptures encourage us to continue growing in knowledge of Christ?

Ephesians 3:16-19

John 14:15-17; 23-27

John 15:12-16

John 17:20-23

How has your life changed since you invited Jesus to come into your life?

On the cover of this study there are several illustrations of some of the countless gifts we receive when we become a child of God. We have not used these specific words before but let's look at them and what they mean. Most of these words are taught in the book of Romans and they will be studied in more detail later.

First, let's consider the meaning of "redeemed". Before we receive forgiveness for our sin we are doomed to pay its penalty. When Christ paid our sin debt on the cross he proclaimed it was "paid in full".

One of the statements Christ made from the cross ("Tetelestai") meant "the debt is paid". When Christ died, all of your sins were future tense. (See Romans 3:24; Galatians 2:20). You no longer need to carry the guilt of your past and the sin for which Christ died. When you as a child of God receive his payment for sin you are set free from the penalty of all your sin, past, present, and future. That's what it means to be "redeemed".

Next, let's consider the title, "joint heir". Since we are adopted into the family of God, we have all the privileges and authority that go with that position. He is our "Abba Father". We are accepted into His Family not on the basis on what we have done but on whose we are. (We will discuss this more in the next chapter when we study about his unconditional love. For additional reading now, see Romans 8:16-17).

Thirdly, let's look at the meaning of "justified". We have studied quite a bit about justification but we haven't used that specific word before. Because Christ not only dealt with our sin problem He erased it as though it had never happened. Now when God looks at us He sees the blood of Christ which has covered us and washed our sins away. He sees us "just-as-if-I'd" never sinned. (Romans 5:1,5,9)

When the full impact of that fact from God's Word is understood we won't ever be the same. We will have a new freedom in Christ – not TO sin but to choose NOT to sin! Sin's power has been broken! Instead of having a license to sin our heart's desire is changed. We will want to show God's love through an obedient life! This is truly good news! It's also evidence of beginning to understand the grace and mercy of God.

In the following chapters we will go over the remainder of the meanings of the words in the illustration on the cover. An additional study of each of these words on your own will always be beneficial as you grow in God's grace and Christlikeness.

For God so loved the world that he gave his one and only Son, that whoever believes in him shall not perish but have eternal life.
John 3:16 (NIV)

4. Understanding His Love

What is God really like?

The entire Bible teaches who God is. His attributes are those descriptive terms of His nature. This limited study cannot even begin to touch on His awesome majesty and power, or His love. He is just. He is holy. He is Almighty. He is Creator. He is omnipresent (everywhere), He is omnipotent (all powerful). He is omniscient (all knowing).

There is no way that we, as finite humans, can ever fully understand the complexity of the nature of God. One of His attributes is love. One of the basic needs of every person is to feel loved. God's love is unconditional. It is sacrificial. It is unending. In our human relationships sometimes love is based on performance or devotion. Therefore, it's hard to understand how a Holy God could love us unconditionally with all the bad (evil) things that we have said or done.

So often our perceived value as a human being is based on what we're paid in a particular job. When we understand our immense worth as individuals, loved by God, it makes a huge difference in our self-esteem. We are loved by God because it is His nature to love, not because we deserve it or earn it. He left heaven and endured the cross for each of us because of who He is!

As humans, though, we all fail. We sin. The Bible teaches that "All have sinned, and come short of the glory of God." (Romans 3:23. NIV). The words "come short" in the original language mean that we all "miss the target." The picture here is of an arrow being shot from a bow, falling short of the target. The target represents holiness or sinlessness. Some of us may make it closer to the target than others, but the Scripture says, we all sin, none of us can hit the target. What is so amazing is that we can come to God just as we are. We don't have to clean up our life first. That's His job. Our job is to let Him be the boss of our life.

Romans 3:10 says, "There is none righteous (sinless). No not one."

So, how can Jesus Christ love sinful people, like you and me? This writer cannot understand that! I'm just overwhelmingly grateful that He does!

Let these words penetrate your soul: *Jesus loves you so much that, if you were the only person on Earth, He would have left Heaven, come to Earth to die for you and pay for your sins.*

Personalize the words of this song that most of us have heard all our life, written by Anna B. Warner:

> "Jesus loves **me**, this I know, For the Bible tells me so.
> Little ones, to Him belong. They are weak, but He is strong.
> Yes, Jesus loves **me**! Yes, Jesus loves **me**!
> Yes, Jesus loves **me**! The Bible tells me so."

Do you believe that this unconditional love can be yours? Do you understand that God's love is not based on your works and you can't do anything to deserve it? God's love can reach the vilest sinner that has ever lived. No thief, prostitute, murderer, adulterer, rapist, or homosexual, is beyond the reach of God's redeeming, unconditional love. Neither are YOU!

ZACCHAEUS, CHOSEN AND LOVED BY GOD

When Jesus was walking the Earth, some of the most hated men were the tax collectors. They often charged more for taxes than was due, therefore they were often wealthy and despised. Let's look at the way Jesus interacted with one notorious tax collector by the name of Zacchaeus.

Read Luke 19:1-10

How does the story of Zacchaeus illustrate God's love for sinners?

How did the love of Jesus change Zacchaeus?

THE SAMARITAN WOMAN, CHOSEN AND LOVED BY GOD

One of the customs in the day of Jesus was for women to gather at the local well. We find in the Gospel of John the account of a Samaritan woman who came to the well, apparently alone, wanting to avoid the condescending eye of others. Apparently her reputation was questionable and well known. Samaritans were looked down upon by the Jews because they were a mixed race. Often Jews would travel many miles out of the way to avoid going through Samaria. When Jesus approached her she was surprised because it was obvious He was a Jew. Customarily a Jewish man would not speak to a Samaritan woman, especially one with a questionable reputation.

Read John 4:1-42

How does the meeting of Jesus with the Samaritan woman at the well illustrate God's unconditional love?

Jesus knew that this woman was an adulteress. Why do you think that Jesus asked her to "Go, call your husband and come back" in verse 16?

How did the unconditional love of Jesus change the Samaritan woman?

Complete these thoughts in your journal:

I am fully pleasing to God because:
I am totally forgiven by God because:
I am unconditionally loved by God because:

When we experience God's love, we are enabled to love others as He does. On our own this isn't possible but, as we mature as children of God, His love flows through us and is seen in us by others.

4. Understanding His Love

1. Spend some time alone with God. Open your heart to Him.
2. Practice the awareness of His Presence.
3. Speak words out loud of love to Him.
4. Ask Him to help you to love others as He loves you.
5. Look at the topic of "God's Love" in the back of your church hymnal. Read the words that godly men and women have written in hymns that speak of the love of God. A great one to begin with is "The Love of God" by Frederick M. Lehman. Pay close attention to the second verse. Other hymns with great messages are "My Savior's Love" and "No One Ever Cared for Me Like Jesus".

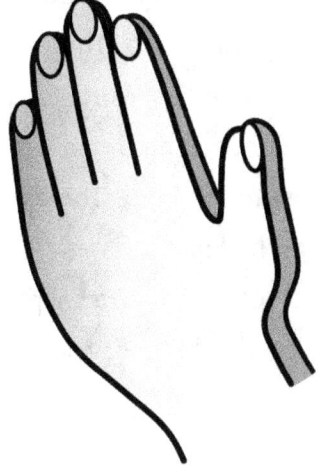

Devote yourselves to prayer, being watchful and thankful. And pray for us, too, that God may open a door for our message.
Col. 4:2-3

5. How Do I Talk to You?

Lord, Teach Me to Pray

The disciples asked Jesus to teach them to pray. What is prayer? How do we know what to pray? We may feel awkward at first when we begin to pray, especially when we pray out loud. However, with time, it will be as natural as breathing. Prayer, simply speaking, is spiritual breathing or fellowshipping with God.

In many religions, and sometimes even in Christianity, prayers are recited. They become a formality with little thought about the meaning of the words, or to whom they are spoken. "Now I lay me down to sleep..." etc. is often one of the first prayers we learn.

When we examine the prayers in the Bible, they are always spontaneous and expressions from the heart. Prayer involves communicating with God from our hearts, and learning to listen to Him speak to us. He does this through His Spirit and through His Word. So, prayer is essential to grow in the knowledge of Christ. King David wrote down many of his prayers which he also sang to the Lord. These are found in the book of Psalms, in the middle of the Bible.

Choose from this list of Psalms and read the entire chapter aloud! Reading a Psalm aloud every day is a good habit to develop.

Write this list in your notebook for future reference:

Psalm 20	Psalm 24	Psalm 32	Psalm 34
Psalm 51	Psalm 57	Psalm 102	Psalm 139
Psalm 147	Psalm 150		

In the Bible the disciples asked Jesus to teach them to pray. Spontaneous praying, though needs little instruction. When we cry out to God from a heart that is seeking Him – God hears us.

At times, praying seems tedious because of the lies of the enemy. The enemy wants us to doubt that God is listening to our prayer, especially if it seems our prayer is not immediately answered. Spending consistent time with God in prayer every day is work. It requires discipline and instruction. For that reason it is often neglected. Yet this is where the power to live the Christian life is developed, in the "prayer closet" alone with God.

When the disciples asked Christ to teach them to pray He responded with the "Model Prayer."

5. How Do I Talk to You?

Read Matthew 6: 9-13 and answer the following questions in your notebook:

    How did God want the disciples to approach him when they prayed?

    Is it necessary to acknowledge who God is when we pray?

    Should we be submissive when we pray?

    What did Jesus ask the disciples to pray for?

One of the most touching passages in the Bible is the prayer that Jesus prayed for us, his children, before he went to the cross. It's found in the gospel of John.

Read John 17:1-26

    What was Christ's desire in verse 1?

    What was his stated purpose for coming to earth?

    What did Jesus request the Father to do?

    What did he pray for his disciples?

    What did he pray for other followers?

When we examine prayers in the Bible we discover that many of them have certain subjects or elements in them. Though not all prayers include these, it is helpful when we are learning to pray to be aware of them and let them be our guide.

SUBJECTS TO INCLUDE IN YOUR PRAYERS:

1. Adoration/Praise: Words like "Lord". "Our Father" (Acknowledge His attributes.)
2. Thanksgiving: "Thank you for …… (Your blessings)"
3. Confession: "Forgive me for ….."
4. Petition: "Help me ……"
5. Intercession: "I pray for ….." (Other people and their needs)
6. Close in "Jesus name". (He's our Intercessor.)

Developing a system or organization to our prayer life is sometimes helpful. Keeping your prayer requests organized will be a blessing to you and others as you see God answer your prayers through the years. Some people keep a prayer journal or use a system that others have developed. The local Christian bookstore is a wonderful source for these. For some of us, assigning a specific category for intercession, some as daily (ie. personal and family needs, revival in America) and some as weekly proves helpful.

For example:

Sunday - Church Services and Staff
Monday – Missionaries and Christian ministries
Tuesday – Tasks that God has given me
Wednesday – World leaders and our elected officials
Thursday – Those sick and in need
Friday – Family and Friends
Saturday – Sinners and the unsaved

We've already discussed the importance of spending time alone with God. It's important though that we don't become legalistic and feel guilty if we aren't consistent. I'm sure you've heard the phrase "life happens." That's so true. Our normal schedule of activity may sometimes be interrupted. All of us face the challenge of being consistent in our time alone with God.

Sometimes we must be flexible and realize God understands. However, discipline in private worship is important because it is our private time with God Almighty and it's precious to God. We should not let legalism (an over emphasis of the method used) rob us of the joy of knowing Him intimately and spending time with Him. Intimacy in worship is the ultimate experience of the believer. Adoration and praise are what escort us to the very Presence of God. As we focus on His attributes and bask in who He is, our spirits are renewed and joy floods our soul.

Our prayer time should be flexible, be open and honest, and be submissive. When it is, we will be blessed! Practice an awareness of His Presence at other times as well. That's what is meant by "Pray without ceasing." Walk (moment by moment) in an attitude of prayer.

This doesn't mean we look sad and sober. On the contrary, we should "rejoice evermore" (1 Thessalonians 5: 16) in all circumstances, living above them as we're aware of His continuing presence. Is it easy to obey this verse? Absolutely NOT!

In the midst of fear, adversity, failures, disappointments, etc. we must choose to rejoice! Our will is what we choose to exercise at this point, not our feelings! We, as an act of our will, choose to rejoice, though we may not feel joyful.

Often we do experience a feeling of JOY in the middle of pain and suffering when we have spent the necessary time praying. God has a way of changing us in the midst of the circumstance, though the circumstance doesn't change.

Sometimes believers find that praying aloud and singing praises in solitude (or the car) are ways they first learn to worship. (This is not recommended if you are the driver and traffic is an issue! However it does provide a certain freedom of expression that we might not want other humans to hear!)

In the spirit realm the angels may be singing along if we need help to stay on tune! Learning to express oneself freely to God is rewarding and freeing to our Spirit! Singing short choruses of praise is a great way to start worshipping the Lord. Singing along with a Christian radio station is a good place to begin.

PRAYING IN GOD'S WILL

Sometimes friends and family and people at church may ask us to pray for things that are difficult to understand. We may not recognize what God is doing and knowing His will in certain situations is challenging. Natural disasters and human tragedies are unexplainable. It's not uncommon for mature believers to question why God allows things to happen. Sometimes a certain situation from the way we see it, just doesn't make sense. In the course of time we may begin to understand why God allowed the circumstance to happen.

We can be sure that God's will never contradicts the principles in His Word. His promises are true. He is always faithful to provide grace in all situations. There is guidance in God's Word to help us pray prayers that are in His will.

Read the following Scriptures and summarize what you have learned, paying close attention to the context and the prayer requests:

2 Chronicles 7:14

Ezra 8:21-23

Psalm 6:2-3

Romans 8:26-30,34

JESUS, OUR EXAMPLE IN PRAYER

You might think that because Jesus was God he wouldn't need to pray. However, that's not the case. He often found a solitary place to spend time with the Father.

Read the following passages and take notes of when and where Jesus prayed.

Mark 1:35

Matthew 14:23

Luke 6:12

Luke 4:1-2

John 17

Matthew 26:39-44

"Learning to pray"
by Alfred, Lord Tennyson

More things are wrought by prayer
Than this world dreams of.
Wherefore, let thy voice
Rise like a fountain for me night and day.
For what are men better than sheep or goats
That nourish a blind life within the brain,
If, knowing God, they lift not hands of prayer
Both for themselves and those
Who call them friends?

THOUGHT TO PONDER

List some specific ways to improve your time alone in prayer.

How is public or group praying different from private prayer? Should it be?

What do these verses say about precautions that should be taken when praying in public?

Mark 11.25

1 Peter 3:7

(In our quiet time we should meditate on God's thoughts in His Word, not our own thoughts.)

*Let us draw near to God with a sincere heart
in full assurance of faith...*
Hebrews 10:22a

6. Experiencing His Presence

His Awesomeness!

Have you ever been overwhelmed with God's Presence? Have you ever seen a beautiful sunset or listened to the sounds of nature and sensed God was there? Have you ever knelt in brokenness over your sin or family needs and felt Him there? Have you needed to earnestly intercede for a fellow believer or friend and God was there?

The awareness of God's Presence is the beginning of worship. Communing with the Lord and worshiping Him is a privilege that only God's children can experience. His power is released when worship takes place.

We may attend church regularly and never truly worship. Because God is omnipresent, meaning He is everywhere, our communication with Him may take place anywhere we happen to be. Worship can take place anytime your heart is in tune with His. It may be on the beach, or a mountaintop, or beside a quiet stream. It is a common misconception that worship must include certain church rituals and ceremonies. You can worship alone, in any quiet setting with just you and God. In contrast, worship can also take place in the midst of celebration and praise in a huge congregation.

Read David's psalm in **1 Chronicles 16:7-36**.

Compare the above passage to **Psalm 105; Psalm 96; Psalm 106:1, 47-48**.

What did you discover?

Isaiah 55:6 commands us to "seek the Lord while He may be found." The enemy tries to hinder us from experiencing God's Presence. He tempts us through our own weakness, and through the hindrances and distractions of our flesh. Sometimes we let concern over what others think of us (pride) keep us from freely worshipping.

There is no higher privilege that is ours as His children, than to worship Him. There is nothing that blesses the heart of God as does our worship.

What do these Scriptures tell us about worship?

Exodus 20:4

I Chronicles 16:23-25; 29

I Chronicles 29:10-20

Psalm 95:6

John 4:24

Romans 12:1

Prayer, praise, and worship are essentials to living a victorious Christian life. These are as breathing is to us physically. Remember, prayer is "spiritual breathing." There is no power in our life if there is no prayer. When we do pray we find the posture of the heart, more than our physical posture, is what is important.

When we approach God in reverence, we can also approach Him with confidence through the blood of Christ. The Bible says in Hebrews 4:16 "Let us then approach the throne of grace with confidence, that we may receive mercy and find grace to help us in our time of need." At times we may go through periods of testing. During those times, seasons of prayer and fasting make spiritual giants of us. They grow us in the faith.

MAKING HIS RICHES MINE

Did you know that you are RICH? Not with a big bank account or fancy cars or a big house. Rather where it really matters! Earthly riches are short lived but our riches in Christ will last forever! What are they? When you became His child what did He give you?

Do you understand your privileges and your value?

Remember—if you were the only person alive, Jesus would have come to the cross to die just for you!

The heart of our study is found in the next few pages. Spend time meditating on these following truths and ask God to increase your understanding of each one. It's important to repeat this prayerfully until the full impact of it begins to sink into your spirit. It's by no means a complete list of all that God has done for us but it's a start! You may not understand the profoundness of what you are speaking but God knows and both you and He will be blessed!

Before you make this part of your quiet time on a regular basis you may want to take one statement and Scripture each day and read the Scripture context. Take notes on what you learn.

SPEAK TO GOD ALOUD AND DECLARE THESE TRUTHS FROM SCRIPTURE

- I am born again by the blood of the Lamb. (Romans 5:9; Ephesians 1:7)
- My sins are washed away in the blood of the Lamb. (John 1:29)
- I am in the Lamb of God who takes away the sin of the world. (Ephesians 1:4)
- I am born again by the incorruptible Word of God, that lives and abides forever (1 Peter 1:23)
- I am a new creation in Christ Jesus, old things are passed away, and all things are become new. (2 Corinthians 5:17)
- I was chosen in Christ Jesus before the foundation of the world. (Ephesians 1:4)
- I am accepted in the Beloved. (Ephesians 1:4-6)
- I am sealed with the Holy Spirit unto the Day of Redemption. (Ephesians 1:13)
- I am reconciled to God, through the blood of the cross. (Romans 5:10)
- I am justified, declared righteous in Christ Jesus. (Romans 5:1,9)

- I have been crucified with Christ. (Galatians 2:20; Romans 6:4, 11)
- I have been resurrected with Christ. (Galatians 2:20; Romans 6:4, 11)
- I am seated with Christ in heavenly places. (Ephesians 1:3)
- Christ, who is above all demonic principalities and powers, lives in me. (Ephesians 1:21)
- I am more than a conqueror through Christ who loves me. (Romans 6:14,22; 8:37)
- I have the mind of Christ. (I Corinthians 2:16)
- I am the bride of Christ. (Revelation 22:17)
- I am the holy temple of God. Christ lives in me. (Colossians 1:27)
- I am an heir of God and a joint heir with Jesus Christ. (Ephesians 2:11; Romans 8:17)
- My citizenship is in heaven. My name is written in the Lamb's Book of Life. (Ephesians 2:6)
- Nothing can separate me from the love of Christ Jesus my Lord. (Romans 8:38-39)
- I am God's purchased possession; bought by the blood of the Lamb; sealed by the Holy Spirit. (Ephesians 1:13-14)
- I am God the Father's love gift to His Son. (Ephesians 1:14)
- God is my Father (Romans 8:15).
- Jesus is my Savior (Hebrews 9:28; Ephesians 2:8-9). Jesus is my Lord (John 11:27). Jesus is my intercessor (Hebrews 12:24). Jesus is my advocate (Hebrews 12:14-15). Jesus is my great High Priest (Hebrews 10:12; 9:11). Jesus is my Great Shepherd (Psalm. 23; Isaiah 40:11). Jesus is my coming King (Hebrews 9:28).

MY POSITION: STAND FIRM, SURRENDERED TO HIS LORDSHIP

- I take my stand within the veil, in the Holy of Holies. (2 Corinthians 3:12-18)
- I lay aside every weight of sin. (Hebrews 12:1; I John 1:9)
- Search me, O God, and know my heart, Try me and know my thoughts and see if there be any wicked way in me. (Psalm 139:23-24)
- I acknowledge my transgressions. I acknowledge my sin unto Thee, my iniquity I will not hide. (Psalm 51)
- Purge me with hyssop and I will be clean. Wash me and I shall be whiter than snow. (Psalm 51)
- Create in me a clean heart O God, renew a right spirit within me. (Psalm 51)
- Restore unto me the joy of Thy salvation. (Psalm 51)
- I bring every thought into the obedience of Christ. (2 Corinthians 10:5)
- I cast down strongholds and every imagination that exalts itself against Christ. (1 Corinthians 10:4)
- I take the whole armor of God. (Ephesians 6:11)
    1. The girdle of truth
    2. The breastplate of righteousness
    3. The sandals of the Gospel of peace
    4. The shield of faith with which I quench the firey darts of the devil.
    5. The Sword of the Spirit, the Word of God
    6. The canopy of prayer

- I overcome the Devil with the blood of the Lamb, the word of my testimony. (Revelation 12:11)
- I stand with the Lord of Hosts in the warfare against the enemy. The battles are His. He teaches my hands to war. He leads me in continual triumph. (Psalm 18:34)
- I stand in God, my High Tower, my Refuge, my Fortress, under the shadow of the Almighty (Psalm 91:1; 2 Samuel 22:3)
- I overcome through Jesus Christ. I overcome fear, timidity, unbelief, doubt, disease, death, the world, the flesh, and the Devil. (I John 2:12-14)
- I press on toward the mark of the upward calling of God in Christ Jesus. (Philippians 3:14)
- I reckon myself to be dead indeed unto sin, but alive unto God through Jesus Christ our Lord. (Romans 6:11)

GIVE HIM PRAISE

As we've done before in our private worship, speak Scriptures aloud of praise to God. Use a version that speaks to your heart. Here are some suggestions:

- "Thou are worthy O Lord to receive glory and honor and power and riches and wisdom and strength and blessing." (Revelation 4:11)
- "Thine O Lord, is the greatness, and the power, and the glory, and the victory, and the majesty; for all that is heaven and the earth is Thine: Thine is the kingdom, O Lord, and Thou art exalted as head above all." (1 Chronicles 29:10-13)
- "Bless the Lord, O my soul, and all that is within me, bless His holy name." (Psalm 103:1)

- "Bless the Lord, O my soul; and forget not all His benefits; who forgiveth all thine iniquities; who healeth all thy diseases; who redeemeth thy life from destruction, who crowneth thee with loving kindness and tender mercies; who satisfieth thy mouth with good things so that thy youth is renewed like the eagles." (Psalm 103:1-5)

- "O God, thou art my God; early will I seek Thee; my soul thirsteth for Thee, my flesh longeth for Thee in a dry and thirsty land, where there is no water, to see Thy power and Thy glory. Thy loving kindness is better than life. My lips shall praise Thee, I will bless Thee while I live. I will lift up my hands in Thy name." (Psalm 63:1-4)

- "Praise Thee O Lord, my Father; who heals the broken hearted, binding up their wounds. Who opens the eyes of the blind to see, who opens my ears to hear Thy voice. Who floods my barren desert with water. Who gives me the song in the night. Who shatters the darkness with the light of thy Presence. Who walks and talks with me along the way. Who speaks to me when I sin, leading me to confession and cleansing. Who fills my heart with laughter, and my lips with praise." (Isaiah 61:1; Psalm 126:2)

- "Thou art my Great Shepherd. I am the sheep in Your flock." (Psalm 23; Jeremiah 31:10)

- "I extol Thee. I adore and worship Thee. I praise Thee." (Psalm 145)

6. Experiencing His Presence

"Hearing His Word"
by Gregory of Naziarus

Lord, as I read…
Let me hear you singing.
As I read your words,
Let me hear you speaking.
As I reflect on each page,
Let me see your image.
As I seek to put your precepts into practice,
Let my heart be filled with joy.

All Scripture is God-breathed and is useful for teaching, rebuking, correcting, and training in righteousness, so that the man of God may be thoroughly equipped for every good work.
2 Tim. 3:16-17 (NIV)

7. My Blueprint For Life

God's Love Letter

Since this study began, our familiarity with God's Word has grown. We realize it truly is God's love letter to His children. Though it's often read and scoffed at by unbelievers we look to it as our blueprint for life. The sacredness (divinely inspired), totality (completeness), and inerrency (accuracy) of the Scripture is essential to our fundamental belief. It is the primary way that God speaks to us as individuals. Many martyrs have given their lives because they refused to denounce its truth. Its existence in the form we have today, kept through all these years, is truly a miracle of God.

The belief in the totality of the Scripture is important because there are many religions who have their own holy writings. We as Christians believe that the Bible is the only sacred writings of our Faith.

The Bible provides lessons from the lives of men and women in the past, it is a blueprint for our lives today and it also gives us a glimpse into eternity. It is where we discover the true spiritual riches that are ours as God's children.

There are five methods of studying the Bible. Most churches offer Bible Study in special classes. These can be extremely beneficial to glean the deeper truths in God's Word. In addition to group studies, our own personal study allows God to speak to us individually in order to share truths that He has for us.

Pastors and teachers share with us what God has taught them. Some pastors teach "precept upon precept." In other words, they teach a book of the Bible, continuing from week to week. Hearing the Word is important to our growth but hearing is only one of the following 5 methods of study. All five are important in order to mature as a believer in Christ.

FIVE METHODS OF BIBLE STUDY

1. Listening to God's Word

The Spirit-filled believer will look forward to hearing from God's Word just as a hungry person looks forward to a great meal. The Bible is God's nourishment for the soul. Godly pastors and teachers share insights into God's Word that increase our faith. Establishing the habit of attending a weekly Bible Study will not only inspire us, but feed us principles that we can apply to our lives. (If the church you attend is focused on social issues more than teaching the Bible, you may want to look for another church.)

 *Read and paraphrase Romans 10:17*

2. Reading the Bible

Just as physical nourishment is needed daily, so spiritual nourishment is needed daily as well. A systematic reading of the Bible should be part of the daily spiritual exercise. Some people like to read through the Bible in a year. Others read a chapter in Proverbs, Psalms and the New Testament everyday. Others do in-depth studies of a specific book each year. Whatever God leads you to do, remember consistency is the key to growth.

 *Read and paraphrase Deuteronomy 17:19-20*

(Suggested reading order: John, 1 John, Romans, Luke, Acts, Ephesians, Philippians, Colossians, Mark, 1 Thessalonians, 1 & 2 Corinthians, Galatians, 2 Thessalonians, Matthew, James, 1 & 2 Timothy, Titus, Philemon, 1 & 2 Peter, Hebrews, 2 & 3 John, Jude, Revelation)

3. Personal Study

Taking the time to glean hidden truths of the Scripture is rewarding to the believer. In-depth Bible study is where nuggets of truth are found. It is here that one develops spiritual insights that a casual reader does not see. There are several approaches to Bible Study that will help your individual study time take on new meaning.

 *Read and paraphrase 2 Timothy 2:15*

4. Memorizing Scripture Verses

God's Word enables us to stand against the enemy with the sword of the Spirit. Whenever we are tested and our faith is tried, we can readily recall God's promises that will strengthen us. Memorized Scripture is one of the most powerful resources that we have as believers.

 *Read and paraphrase Psalm 119:9-11*

5. Meditating on Scriptures

After we've studied and/or memorized a passage, it's always beneficial to keep reviewing it for additional insights. The Jews wore Scriptures on their wrists and foreheads to help them remember them. The visual picture of meditation as taught in the Bible is the "chewing of food" over and over, as a cow would chew her cud. So, we are to continue to think over the meaning of Scriptures that God brings to us in our study time, until we've learned the lesson He has for us.

7. MY BLUEPRINT FOR LIFE

Read and paraphrase Psalm 1:2-3
Read and paraphrase Proverbs 7:1-3

One way to be sure that we are praying according to God's will is to pray Scripture into our own life and into the lives of others. There are many promises and prayers in the Scriptures that are wonderful to see come to fulfillment as we pray them into the lives of our loved ones.

FOR ADDITIONAL GROWTH:

Pray aloud that these passages will become reality in someone's life by inserting his or her name in the prayers:

1. Ephesians 3:16-19
2. Ephesians 5:1-2
3. Colossians 1:9-12
4. Romans 12:1-2
5. Isaiah 41:10
6. 2 Timothy 1:7
7. 1 Peter 1:7
8. Philippians 4:6-8

SCRIPTURES TO MEMORIZE:

Write these references in your notebook and start a system of memorization. As God brings other important verses to your attention add them to your list with the goal of memorizing them. You may want to include

it in the section you already have of Scripture promises and you may want to include these promises in your memorization list.

Psalm 139:23-24
Isaiah 26:3; 40:31; 41:10
Jeremiah 29:11
John 6:47
Romans 3:23; 5:8; 6:23; 8:1-2; 10:9-10; 12:1-2
Galatians 2:20
Ephesians 1:18; 2:10
Philippians 1:6; 4:8
Colossians 1:27; 2:6-7
1 Peter 1:3-4
2 Timothy 1:7
1 John 1:9; 3:1

UNDERSTANDING SCRIPTURE

As a new believer, having confidence in your ability to study Scripture for yourself may be lacking. You may feel overwhelmed when you read parts of the Bible, especially the Old Testament and Revelation. Remember, we are finite humans who are all limited in our understanding of such an awesome God and His Word. Also, remember however, as a child of God, you have the same Holy Spirit as any biblical scholar.

With the Holy Spirit as your Teacher, you can learn to interpret and apply the Scriptures to your life. As you mature in your understanding, God may open a door of ministry for you to share with others what you have learned. If so, here are some helpful principles to remember.

When we study a section of Scripture there are several approaches that we can take.

First, if you can, in your mind, go back to literature class in school. Think about the many types of literature: poetry, history, law, etc. Look at the study helps in your Bible, often found in the introduction to a given book. Sometimes it will tell you the type of literature that you are reading. For example, Psalms is poetry that was often sung. Exodus is considered "law" and Romans is "doctrine."

The Old Testament was originally written in Hebrew, the New Testament was originally written in Greek. An early English translation of the Bible was the King James Version. It is sometimes more difficult for us to understand because it was written in English as it was used 400 years ago. Because we don't speak that way in today's culture, other versions have been translated. Often, these are from more accurate manuscripts, and in today's vernacular.

If you have a study Bible, there will usually be footnotes and chain references which take you to other related verses for additional study. Both a lexicon and a concordance can assist you as well. Understanding the tense of the verbs in the original language helps to clarify the meaning. It's also helpful to understand the literary devices, such as metaphors, parables, etc. that are being used. You may want to notice repeated words, and phrases, and purpose clauses in a passage. Some of these clauses may include words like "because," "so that," and "therefore."

Sometimes it will help to list the statements and questions of the main characters and examine how their experiences and their understanding changed. Discovering what they learned about God can help us learn as well.

If you are studying history, like the book of Acts, notice the events that are mentioned. Events in the Bible are part of history. Historians have validated biblical events from the beginning. If you are a history buff, reading other historical accounts may be helpful in acquiring an understanding of the culture of the day in which the author wrote. To ignore the historical circumstances is to remain ignorant of the questions and issues that the author faced.

Our understanding is critical before we apply the passage to our own day. History is not applied in the way a doctrinal letter would be, as when Paul wrote to the Early Church. We also need to look at the larger context. To better understand a passage we should determine the meaning of the entire passage before we decide on the meaning of a specific verse. We must interpret the verse in light of all the Scripture on the same subject by the same author.

Ask yourself, "How can this be used in my life?" Be willing to apply what the teaching says. Does it increase my faith, my commitment, or spur me to action?

When should we take a Scripture literally and when should we look at it figuratively? What do we mean by examining the literal meaning? We take the meaning as it appears at the surface without looking for deeper meanings. Keeping Scripture in context helps to decide whether the passage should be interpreted figuratively or literally.

Normally, it's preferred to take it literally unless the context suggests otherwise. It's also helpful to notice how figures of speech are used. This is opposite of the literal approach. It looks for a deeper or symbolic meaning. Jesus often used metaphors like salt and light to symbolize deeper meanings. (John 16:25)

Determine if every detail has a figurative meaning, as in an allegory. The Parable of the Sower is an example. Jesus interprets the different kinds of soil as different kinds of people.

Read this parable in Matthew 13. Write what you discover in your notebook.

QUESTIONS TO ASK YOURSELF:

When we hear someone teach the Bible, pay close attention to what he or she is saying. Teachers of God's Word are held to a high standard by Scripture. Studies like this are as well. This is why you are encouraged to open God's Word and to examine it for yourself and apply the following principles in order to prove what has been written here. (Read 2 Timothy 2:15)

Ask yourself:
- Is the teacher being consistent with and not contrary to the rest of the Bible?
- Is the interpretation consistent with the character of God?
- Is the passage kept in context?
- Does the Spirit confirm the interpretation as you continue to pray about it?

REMEMBER:

- Our culture is different, therefore we can't always apply the culture of that day to ours.
- We shouldn't twist the meaning of a passage to fit our view point.
- We should always keep Scriptures in the context.
- We should try to understand the meaning (or meanings) in the original language.

"Be still and know that I am God; I will be exalted among the nations, I will be exalted in the earth."
Psalm 46:10

8. How Can I Hear Your Voice?

The "BE-ATTITUDES"

"Whatever is true, whatever is noble, whatever is right, whatever is pure, whatever is lovely, whatever is admirable - if anything is excellent or praiseworthy - think about such things."
Philippians 4:8 (NIV)

Controlling our thought life is necessary to become more like Christ. Sometimes we are not aware of negative thought patterns that bombard us. The enemy uses "Negative Nancys" and "Cranky Craigs" to distract us from God's grace and bring fear, doubt, criticism, and confusion into our lives. Negative news and reality TV may also become addictive traps. It's important as believers to eliminate all immoral or corrupt (critical) influences.

Listening to Christian music, including hymns, psalms, and spiritual songs, contributes to a positive environment and a healthy mind. Praise is an overflow of His Spirit within us.

 *Look up Ephesians 5:19-20 and Colossians 3:15-17 and note how they are similar.*

Having a thankful and joyful heart are evidences of the fullness of His Spirit. Even if you have never sung except in the car or the shower, you can raise your voice in praise to God. The Holy Spirit lives in you to help you! He also helps you in your thought life. As we've learned already, He comes to live in us when we invite Christ into our life. As we continually surrender our will to His will, our mind will be under His control.

Romans 8:5 says, "Those who live according to the sinful nature have their minds set on what that nature desires; but those who live in accordance with the Spirit have their minds set on what the Spirit desires."

The Holy Spirit is the One who works in us to give us the mind of Christ. This is a process that will continue until we go to be with the Lord in Heaven. Being consistent in God's Word and prayer makes the Holy Spirit's work much easier.

READ PHILIPPIANS 2:1-11

In verse 5 Paul encourages us again to "let" Christ's mind and attitude be ours. If this weren't possible then we would not be asked to do it. It must, therefore, be possible to have the mind of Christ. This is an evidence of spiritual maturity.

In this passage we also see that being obedient to God's Word and having the attitude of a servant, are also evidences of humility and spiritual maturity. (Verse 7) Pride and self-centeredness are opposites of humility and unselfishness and indicate a life not surrendered to the Lordship of Christ.

In these verses we see Christ's example of humility and service. There is no exercise that demonstrates humility more than voluntary fasting. This requires self-denial of one of the most fundamental physical needs. When health allows it, periods of fasting can be extremely beneficial in order to understand His mind, and determine His will and direction in life.

Look up all the Scriptures from your concordance on fasting.

List the purpose for fasting in each of your chosen passages.

What did you learn from this?

GODLINESS

Godliness, holiness, and Christlikeness are words that are seldom heard in church. Yet it is important to understand them. Godliness should be our goal. It is not something that we can achieve on our own. It is rather a divine working of God's Holy Spirit in us as we surrender our will to His will, moment by moment. Christ desires us to be like Him. We become more like Him as we yield to His control.

"No one can be like Jesus like Jesus can." Why is an understanding of this statement so important to the believer?

Who of us is godly? Is it possible for anyone to be godly?

Read Titus 2:11-14.

What did you learn from this passage?

How would you describe a godly person?

Read "The Beatitudes" in Matthew 5:1-12.

Here we find a description of Christ Himself. Which verses present the largest challenges to you?

Look up all the verses in your concordance on godliness. Write a summary of what you learned.

HUMILITY

How would you define humility?

Read 1 Peter 3:8-16

What are the evidences in this passage of a life submitted to God and others?

Jesus is the perfect example of a servant. We cannot follow this example in our own strength. It, also, is a work of His Spirit within us. Servanthood requires thinking of others and their needs first. It means loving unconditionally and being willing to go the "extra mile." These are unnatural to our fleshly instincts

When the Holy Spirit is in control of our lives, His fruit will be seen by others. The fruit of the Spirit is singular. By that we mean if you have one fruit, you will have them all. The Spirit is One Spirit, who is evidenced by all these character qualities.

Read Galatians 5:16-26.

What are the Fruit of the Spirit?

As a child of God you have embarked upon an exciting path. Each day is a gift from God for you to discover His purpose. As you "practice His Presence" continually he will open doors of opportunity to use you to enrich the lives of others. His Spirit will conform you into His image.

Review Chapter 6 of this study often. Remind yourself of who you are in Christ.

WORD STUDIES PRODUCE ADDITIONAL GROWTH (OPTIONAL)

When we surrender our will to His, yield our thoughts to His, and humble ourselves before Him, we can approach His Word and expect to hear His voice. As we wrap up the first part of this study let's apply the principles that we have already learned.

Look up in your concordance one or more of the following words. Beside the word that you want to study in your concordance there will be a list of references from the Bible where the word is used. Look up each one, take notes on the context, notice who is speaking, to whom they are speaking, the circumstance or setting, the time of the writing, etc.

Notice contrasts and similarities from each Scripture and compile lists of them. Spend time meditating about each one and ask God to show you hidden truths that are in the passage.

With these guidelines in mind do word studies on the following:

1) Do a word study on faith. Look up Scriptures. Some questions you may want to answer are: Where does faith come from? How should your faith affect your daily life? How is our faith increased? How is it put into practice daily? (Summarize what you learn.)

2) Do a word study on baptism. What does the word literally mean? Why should we be baptized? What does it symbolize? How is baptism like a wedding ring?

3) Read 2 Timothy 2:20-21. What does it mean to you?

4) Read I Peter 1:18-23 and 2:9-10. What do these verses say about you as a child of God?

Leader Helps
Unit 1

Leaders' Helps

Chapter 1: Thy Word Is Truth

Welcome, leader, to a new study in God's Word that will provide an opportunity to reach others for Christ. This study will affirm that each one who participates has a personal relationship with Christ and will lead them to begin their walk with Him through the basics of Christian growth. It has many potential uses, so be creative!

It's important to relate as much as possible to each person in the group on the first week. Because of this, take the time to greet and get acquainted. Pass around a sheet to acquire names, e-mail, and phone numbers of each one. Ask each person to share his/her name and what they "do on a typical day" and if they are new to the church or group. Be sure to wrap up the greeting time with answering these questions yourself and anything else that you would like to share about yourself so they will get to know you.

Chapter one will be completed in class this first week so pass out books to each one. Since chapter one is about the authority of God's Word there will probably need not be much discussion this first week. Often it takes a few weeks for participants to "free up" to talk. If there are people of other faiths present this will be more challenging.

You may want to encourage them to purchase a study Bible before next week. (If they can't afford it you may want to ask the church for help and provide some copies with a Concordance, chain reference, study helps, etc.)

As you begin you may want to acknowledge that whereas most, if not all of them, believe God's Word is our only inspired revelation of

Scripture, their children and grandchildren may be being taught differently. Other religions have so called "holy writings" (Koran, Book of Mormon", etc.) and so we need to be confident in our understanding that God's Word, the Bible, is the only inspired Word of God.

The Bible is God's revelation of Himself to mankind in written form. It is the basis of all Christian teaching. All other doctrinal studies must be judged by the Bible's content and context. God, in the Person of the Holy Spirit is its Author. He chose humans to pen the words. It's a mystery to us how God can use the finite minds of humans to produce this trustworthy Scripture. Thankfully we don't have to understand it to trust it.

The humans who penned the Scriptures sometimes would do it immediately as the words were given them. At other times there was a delay between the events and the writing them down. God's Spirit led in the timing and accuracy of the writings and inspired the writers at times to memorize passages before they wrote them down.

As the leader of the first week's discussion it is important to lay the foundation for the authority of God's Word as the only source of God's Truth. You may want to review the following passages as you prepare your heart to lead: 2 Peter 1:19-21; 1 Timothy 4:1-5; 2 Timothy 3:14-17; Matthew 5:17-18; 1 Peter 1:24-25; Acts 17:11; Deuteronomy 17:18-20; Isaiah 40:8; Psalm 19:7-10; Psalm 119 (synonyms in this chapter for the Bible: word (29 times), laws (44 times), promise (13 times), decrees (22 times), precepts (21 times), commands (22 times), statutes (22 times), truth (2 times), way (1 time).

Discussion topics:

1. God's Word doesn't attempt to prove God's existence, neither should we attempt to. "The Heavens declare the Glory of God" (Psalm 19:1-4; see also Romans 1:18-20.)

2. Discuss: Proverbs 3:5-6 states "your own understanding" can lead you astray. But God faithfully leads us as we follow Him. His Word guides us. (Psalm 119:105)

3. Sin is not part of other religions in the way that it is in Christianity. God's Word sheds light on our sin throughout Scripture. That's the reason that Christ had to come and die. (Psalm 119:11; Romans 5:8) We owe a sin debt that we cannot pay.

4. In the last question – What do you hope to learn? - ask what they want to learn:

    A. "About God" (ie: a deeper understanding of His love)
    B. About others" (ie: How I can be used to bless others and fulfill my purpose"
    C. About themselves" (ie: To discover hidden sins and habits that rob me of God's peace and plan for my life).

Wrap up the lesson with a reminder that "God's Word is living and active" and the degree to which they open it and actually study it, will they be blessed in this study. (1 Peter 1:23-25; Ephesians 6:16-17; 2 Timothy 1:12-13)

After completing this lesson together, turn to the next lesson. Next week's lesson may help anyone who doubts his/her salvation to settle that doubt, as we discuss "Feelings" and "Faith". Encourage them to invite anyone who struggles with "eternal security" to join the class. (I would recommend closing the class enrollment after the 3rd week to new members.)

Encourage them to set aside about 45 minutes sometime during the week to do the lesson. The more they actually examine the Scriptures, the more they will get out of it.

Share your contact information with them so they can contact you with questions.

Close in Prayer for:

1. God to open the understanding of each one to His Word.
2. They could be consistent in attendance.
3. The attacks of the enemy would be thwarted.

Chapter 2: My New Life in Christ

The verse that introduces this chapter is one that Christ gave in response to Thomas, the disciple's, question, "How can we know the way"? Christ's response must have been a challenge for the disciples to understand, just as it is for many people today. The world often tells us that there are many ways to find truth and many ways to heaven, or eternal life. Jesus was very clear that that is not the case, there is only one way, through Him.

Many people live their lives with doubt, and depend more on their feelings rather than the facts or truth of God's Word. They sometimes fail to exercise faith that simply trusting Christ is enough. At the beginning of the chapter we ask that each person acknowledge that God often uses our feelings to speak to us and cause us to admit we are sinners.

You may have seen a sketch of a train (in Campus Crusade for Christ's "Four Spiritual Laws") that has been used to illustrate this important teaching. The engine is labeled "Facts". The second car is labeled "Faith". The caboose is labeled "Feelings". This illustration helps us understand that the facts of God's Word provide the power to move the train. Faith, or trust in the facts as taught in God's Word, is a gift of God according to Ephesians 4:8-9. Our feelings, or emotions are part of our "heart", where our mind, will, and emotions reside. Our feelings at times are deceptive and can bring doubt and confusion into our lives if we trust in them. In this chapter we want to focus on how God uses our feelings to lead us to himself by helping us to recognize our sin but we must not trust them for assurance of our relationship with Christ. (Here we focus on what faith is, the next chapter will focus more on what faith is not.)

Because the church is where believers and non-believers gather to hear God's Word taught, it's comparable to a hospital where sick people gather to receive treatment. If we attend often, it's likely at some point someone will say something or do something that may offend us. If we allow the enemy to accuse them in our heart we may become discouraged and leave and not come back for a long time, if ever. This is often where our feelings get hurt and we begin to carry a grudge. This may also happen at work, in a club, or even at home. Working on solving challenges in relationships will be the subject of a chapter in the last half of this study.

This chapter encourages each person to admit if they are holding a grudge against someone in the church or elsewhere. Sometimes new believers have unrealistic expectations of people in church. This can be a stumbling block to them. Admitting that we are all sinners is essential to true repentance and trusting Christ's work on the cross for salvation.

Halfway through the chapter each person will be brought to a decision point. They will be asked to confirm their salvation experience. If they are unsure of their relationship with God, they can confess that they are sinners, repent of their sin, pray a prayer of commitment and receive Christ as Savior and Lord. The remainder of the lesson will help them find a healthy church to encourage them to grow spirtually.

As leader, your understanding of the two church ordinances is crucial. They are baptism by immersion (one time, following conversion), and the Lord's Supper (or Communion). Each is to be practiced by the church and is symbolic of the work of Christ in our hearts. Each pictures the death and resurrection of Christ.

Chapter 3: Knowing Whose I Am

As you introduce this lesson, which may be a turning point for some in the class, discuss the statement "We are not sinners because we sin, but rather, we sin because we are sinners" (p. 24). After the discussion, it is suggested that you, or a minister, or deacon, or someone who is experienced in sharing the Gospel, do a demonstration of what an evangelistic team does. Role play going to someone's home and pretend to share the gospel with them. Go through all the steps, including a prayer of commitment. (Allow 20-30 minutes for the demonstration. Helps for this are included in the last chapter of this study.)

As this is happening, God will be able to speak to those in the class. We would hope that each one will be looking inside their hearts to determine who or what they are trusting in for their eternal life. When they completed the lesson at home they saw how in the scriptures many followers started out with sincere questions about who Christ was. They grew in their understanding to the point many eventually recognized Christ as Messiah and Lord. They went from an "intellectual knowledge" of who Christ was (the son of Mary and Joseph of Nazareth) to a heart commitment and trust in Him as Savior and Lord. It is possible some in the class also may have come to recognize for the first time that Christ is the Messiah, who came to take away the sin of the world, including theirs. They may be ready to trust in Him alone for their salvation.

The goal of this lesson is to discover what or who each person is trusting in for their eternal life. We don't want to create doubt but rather settle doubt here. In this chapter we ask questions that will give an opportunity to hear what the person believes. Are they "trying" to be good enough or "doing the best they can" (a works answer – trusting self-effort), trusting in baptism or church membership (again – a works answer), or do they mention what Jesus did for them on the cross? He came to pay our sin debt once for all. He paid the price on the Cross for our sin, thereby providing a way for us to receive the gift of eternal life.

In closing, review what was discussed earlier about our nature to sin and our sin being the reason Christ came to die. Once we have repented of our sin and we have invited Jesus into our lives, the Holy Spirit begins to lead us and teach us truths from the Scriptures. One of the most important truths is found in John 3:16: "For God so LOVED the world, that He gave His only begotten Son…" Our lesson next week is on Christ's unconditional love for us.

Close with this illustration: "Believers live in Christ much like fish live in water. He is our natural element – the Water of Life. Salvation means being "in Christ", asking him for life and living out the life available only in Him". (Taken from "Disciple's Study Bible", Holman Publishers.)

Chapter 4: Understanding His Love

Suggestion to begin the Class – Consider having someone sing a hymn about the love of God. Music speaks to our hearts sometimes more clearly than written words when it comes to the subject of love.

Discuss how Zaccheus' and the Samaritan woman's understanding of the love of Christ grew.

Discuss the meanings of the three Greek words for "love": Eros, (sexual); Phileo, (brotherly); and Agape. Agape love is the most profound because it attempts to give itself away for the beloved. It wants only what's good for the benefit of its object with nothing desired for itself in return. God's love is an expression of His Grace, totally undeserved.

Close in prayer that Christ's love would flow through each person this week.

Chapter 5: How Do I Talk to You?

The goal for the class in this chapter is to understand that prayer should not be complicated, it is simply having a conversation with God. There is no real formula for prayer but we can look at the prayers in the Bible and apply the format if we want to learn to be more effective in our prayer life. Your goal as a leader should be to actually allow time for the class to discuss what they have learned and then allow time to pray together. Before you do, allow time for petitions (requests) of those in the class. You may want to introduce them to "conversational prayer" which means one person starts praying when another has stopped but hasn't yet closed the prayer. There's no better way to learn to pray than to pray. Studying about prayer is simply not enough.

The prayer "closet" is where we become powerful believers and spiritual warfare takes place. Encourage every class member to set aside a place where they regularly get alone with God to pray. Encourage them also to keep a prayer journal with requests and answers that they have received.

Chapter 6: Experiencing His Presence

Two of the most rewarding experiences a believer can have this side of Heaven are worshiping God and leading someone to a saving knowledge of Christ. There is no greater joy than to be ushered into God's Presence when we praise Him. Experiencing His Presence is life-changing. Praising Him and learning to hear Him speak to us is a privilege. In this chapter we embark on a discovery of some of the gifts, privileges, and riches that were given us when we became a child of God. There are many, many more stated throughout God's Word than are included here, but this is a start.

The assignment is short but the impact will potentially be large. Encourage each person to practice praying out loud and get used to hearing their voice speak to God. Praying the prayers in the Bible are a good way to start if they have never prayed out loud. Emphasize the importance of declaring the truths out loud that are included in the chapter. Come boldly to His throne! He inhabits the praises of His people so don't be surprised if God "shows up".

Chapter 7: My Blueprint For Life

In chapter one we began with the importance of God's Word and the foundation that it provides for doctrinal truth as a whole. In this chapter we want to look a little deeper into how to go about studying it. You, as a leader may want to take to class a variety of study Bibles and devotional books that you have used through the years. Discuss why some have been such a blessing to you. Show how to use a concordance and chain reference.

Remember to discuss the potential of reading online now. Even though this is more convenient and becoming more common, there is no way to underline and mark verses that stand out to you. So, be sure that everyone who wants one has a study Bible in print.

When you discuss the Five Methods of Study be sure to give examples of how God has used memorized Scripture in your life to bring strength, comfort, peace, joy, etc.

Chapter 8:
How Can I Hear Your Voice?

The first half of this study focuses on the reader's vertical relationship with God. The second half will focus on horizontal relationships with others. As we conclude this first half we encourage you as the leader to challenge the participants to continue the habits that they have developed in studying the Bible and praying regularly. As they do they will learn to listen to God when He speaks to them. As they hear and obey, they will grow in their understanding of what it means to walk in the Spirit and have the fruit of the Spirit produced in their life, thereby strengthening their relationships with other believers.

The second half of the book may be finished as a group or each person may want to continue the rest of the study on their own. By now they should be able to do it. May God bless you for your faithfulness in teaching His Word. There is coming soon an additional study of Romans 6-8 on the Spirit-filled life by the same author.

Be Blessed!
Jerri Mason

Part 2

MY RELATIONSHIPS WITH OTHERS

Be kind and compassionate to one another, forgiving each other, just as in Christ God forgave you.
Eph. 4:32 (NIV)

1. Practicing Forgiveness

Sometimes Life Hurts!

When you were a child was someone mean to you? With that question, more than likely someone from your past immediately popped into your mind! When you were a teen, did someone make fun of you, let you down, or reject you? If you're normal, the answer is yes and again, the image of that person popped into your mind. All of us experience rejection in many ways throughout life. Have you ever been fired? Ouch! That really hurts! Have you ever been unemployed for a period of time and your normally healthy self-esteem took a nose dive?

Whether we react or respond gracefully at these times may determine if the circumstance makes us bitter or better. If we blame someone for our misfortune it can make us bitter. Sometimes we even blame God for what is happening to us. If we know that God is all powerful, then we know He can make our circumstance better. We know He can intervene and make our resumé the only one that looks good, or He can send us a check in the mail to pay off all our debts.

Maybe we don't blame God, but we blame the person who has hurt us and we refuse to forgive them. We become angry and resentful. The initial emotion most of us feel when we've been hurt is anger. Depending on our temperament, we may react in different ways. Sometimes an extrovert will lash out and vent the anger immediately and "move on." He may say things that he really doesn't mean in the heat of the moment. At that point the offended becomes the offender. Proverbs 12:18 says "Reckless words pierce like a sword." So, instead of resolving the situation, fuel is added to the fire and the problem can escalate out of control.

Introverts may not react at the time of an offense, but they may hold a grudge for years, sometimes even for a lifetime. Resentment may be just under the surface, and with little encouragement it can express itself in a negative attitude and harsh words. Sometimes bitterness can even result in physical symptoms. The Bible says that "A cheerful heart is good medicine, but a crushed spirit dries up the bones." (Proverbs 17:22)

Forgiving everyone completely who has offended us is a process that can be quite painful. In order to forgive, first we must be willing to examine our attitudes and our heart. We need to ask God to help us recall life experiences that caused us pain. We must first acknowledge the offense. In other words, be specific.

1. Practicing Forgiveness

Sometimes it helps to write down the name of each person and what they did to us. This exercise (to clear our conscience) may bring back deep hurts and buried feelings from years before. Even though this is difficult, it is necessary in order to forgive everyone who has offended us.

1) List each person who has offended you and what they did on a sheet of paper. (This may take several days. Don't rush the process.) When you have written all that you can remember, go on to number 2. Add others to your list as you remember additional offenses.

2) Pray and ask God to give you His grace to forgive them, then choose to forgive them.

Pray a prayer something like this:

"Lord Jesus, I acknowledge that I have not forgiven _____ for the pain and hurt that they caused me. Forgive me for the anger and bitterness that I have felt toward them. I know You have forgiven me for my sin and that You've asked me to forgive others when they sin against me. (Read Mark 11:25) So, in faith, right now, I choose to forgive _____ for _____."

Repeat this process until you've covered all the offenses you can remember. Forgiveness is an act of your will!

Ask God to help you, through His grace, to be able to forget the pain they caused you and to love them as He loves them. Remember – forgiveness is not a feeling. It's a choice, a decision we make! Understand that feelings of forgiveness for the other person may never come.

Often, though, there is a strong emotional release that comes deep in our spirit when we forgive someone. Sometimes people say they felt "like a burden was lifted." There also can be physical evidence that takes place in the body with this release! Others may notice a new radiance in your face! We experience a fresh joy and freedom!

How can we keep this refreshment in our spirit?

By keeping "short accounts" with others. Choose to forgive people immediately when they offend you or make you angry. It's as simple as lifting up a prayer and asking God to take the anger away and to give you an understanding heart. As we practice forgiveness it becomes easier, though it's an exercise none of us will ever be able to master until we get to Heaven. A forgiving heart is a *gift* of God's grace that is worked in us by God as we submit to His Spirit's control of our life.

THOUGHT TO PONDER AND PRAY

In order to clear our conscience, sometimes we need to contact the person that hurt us. We may need to ask them to forgive us for holding a grudge and being bitter toward them. (Note: We should always be discerning here, after much prayer and possible counsel. If you decide that you should go talk with the person, do it in person, or on the phone, NOT in writing or e-mail. Anything in writing can be kept and can continue to be read. This can potentially cause more problems since the person has your confession available to read often. If they weren't aware of how you felt previously it can cause a reaction in them, causing them to sin. It could also present legal concerns in some instances.)

If you decide that God is leading you to go to them, have your spouse (or a friend) go with you when you talk to them. Keep in mind that this could initiate a negative response or cause additional conflicts. You may decide that it's best to keep it between you and God.

God's grace is given us to enable us to forgive. If we tell a friend or spouse about the offense we may cause them to hold a grudge. They may not apply God's grace to the situation and therefore our sharing may cause them to sin. For this reason, we should consider the repercussions before we tell anyone outside of the circle of offense about the situation.

A counselor is the only exception to this. Counselors are trained to listen and give us direction and guidance. If it was a serious hurt and you need guidance in how to resolve an offense, speaking with a counselor may be necessary.

 *Look up the following Scriptures and write them in your notebook. Add them to your list to memorize.*

    1. Ephesians 4:32

    2. Colossians 3:12-13

After you have forgiven all the people on your list, there's one more very important step!

DESTROY THE LIST!

 *Record in your journal how "Practicing Forgiveness" has made a difference in your life.*

Cast all your anxiety on Him because He cares for you.
1 Peter 5:7 (NIV)

2. Emotions in Motion

Who's in Control?

Have you ever seen a train being pulled by a caboose? No! If the caboose is in front, the engine pushes from the back. The train isn't designed to function efficiently this way. The train moves faster and more efficiently when the power source, the engine, is in front. When we allow our feelings to control our life, we may become frustrated, depressed, or out of control, instead of being God controlled.

Sometimes an emotional roller coaster ride may ensue. If this happens other people may go for a ride with us and it can be extremely disruptive and unsettling to a marriage, a home, a friendship, an office, or a church. Sometimes we need to take an emotional step back. It's possible that we need to detach ourselves emotionally from a situation in order to think clearly.

How do we do that? First, we need to surrender our emotions to God's control.

Take some time to get alone with His Word and pray until you have His peace about a matter. Remember, faith (the engine) should be the power that pulls the train of our life. Facts from God's Word are the train cars, the caboose is our feelings. If these get out of order, we may have problems as a result.

From our previous study we know that God's will is not always easy to understand. We also learned that not everything that happens in our life is God's will. When we seek Him in difficult situations He will work "all things for good." (Romans 8:28-30) Even situations that appear evil or bad can be used in our life when we surrender them to Him in faith.

After we have the mind of Christ, His emotions will be our emotions. We will experience peace and the other Fruit of the Spirit as well.

Do your emotions present a challenge to you?

Some common emotions that are hard to control are:

- Fear
- Anger
- Jealousy
- Disappointment

The last one is sometimes overlooked as being a root cause of our problem. However, when we think about it, it may impact us more than we realize.

LIVING WITH DISAPPOINTMENT

Disappointment can be the result of many life experiences. It may come from the loss of a parent, a child, a spouse through separation, death, or divorce. It can also result from a longing for something or someone that we never experience. Dreams and desires may never be realized. Sometimes the pain of our loss can last a lifetime. We may feel helpless to do anything about the situation. There may be no way to change it.

God knows our pain and He understands what we are experiencing. When we go to His Word He will give us comfort and peace. Sometimes that's the last thing we want to do, though. Even mature believers can become depressed and turn away from God and from people who are able and willing to help them. Sometimes anger, guilt, pride, and embarrassment keeps us from being honest with ourselves and others.

All of us experience disappointment. It may be as simple as losing a favorite piece of jewelry, or the loss of a football game. Most parents want to teach their children to learn to "push through" the loss. We want our children to learn from the experience and become better individuals because of it. We sometimes fail to do that when our own disappointments seem like mountains we can't get over.

Let's consider some common disappointments.

Sometimes a couple cannot have a child or their child has a severe disability. This can bring extra stress into the relationship. There's a tendency to play the "blame game" sometimes blaming yourself and at times blaming your spouse. When a couple loses a child, this same pain is felt and the family is never the same. The entire family is shaken to the core.

Sometimes a child is killed or may choose to walk away, like the prodigal son. This brings a void that no one else can fill. Holidays and family events are forever changed.

When any of these occurs, often the pain is deep, and is sometimes too much to endure in one's own strength. Looking at Scripture is beneficial because we can find people there who have experienced what we are experiencing. Bible characters show us God's principles in human experience. We're able to learn from both their good and bad choices, identify with them in the emotions they feel, and in their successes and failures. Organizing our study into a Bible worksheet is a tool that we may want to create to help us learn from a Bible character.

In the Old Testament we find the account of Hannah, who was childless. She had prayed for many years for a child.

READ 1 SAMUEL 1 AND 2 WITHOUT STOPPING

COMPLETE A BIBLE WORKSHEET:
1. Read the Scripture again, and begin to take notes in a notebook of information about Hannah. List everything in quotes that Hannah spoke. Also list the specific verb phrases that note what she did. (ie. "Hannah stood up.")
2. List her various character qualities, flaws, and attitudes.
3. Write down the biblical principles that you see illustrated in Hannah's life. Note the Bible reference for each principle. (Proverbs is a good source for this.)
4. Write down the ways these principles can apply to your life.

Compare what you learned about Hannah to the description of the "virtuous woman" in Proverbs 31:10-31. Summarize what you have learned about these two women.

2. Emotions in Motion

What is the leading lesson taught by Hannah's life?

Read 2 Samuel 19

David was referred to as a "man after God's own heart" yet his loss overwhelmed him. What loss did King David experience?

Read Psalm 66

Where did David find comfort?

Find another Psalm that David wrote to help him overcome depression. Does God always answer the longings and desires of our heart? Why?

How do we find peace and comfort in the midst of disappointments?

DEPRESSION

Disappointment often leads to depression.

What is your definition of depression?

What emotions are referred to in these passages?

I Samuel 1:6 – 7

Proverbs 15:1

Proverbs 15:13

Romans 9:2

2 Corinthians 7:10

What are some of the causes of depression?

Matthew 6:25-34

Ecclesiastes 7:9

2 Timothy 1:7

Psalm 40:12

One definition of depression is "turned in anger." Often this anger is suppressed if we feel guilty about blaming God for our circumstance or our loss. Remember, God's love for you is boundless, eternal, and measureless. He loves you so much He would have died for you alone. Receive His love and grace today. He cares for YOU!

EXPERIENCING VICTORY OVER DEPRESSION:

- Choose to praise the Lord for His goodness. List all your blessings. Isaiah 1:3
- Confess your sins of anger and frustration over your situation. I John 1:9
- Find someone who YOU can help through THEIR tough time. Philippians 2:4
- Give thanks in the midst of your circumstance. I Thessalonians 5:18
- Pray with thanksgiving that God knows and will meet your needs. (Philippians 4:6-7)
- Read God's promises.* Anticipate the super abundant life God has for you. (Psalms 119:59-60)
- Keep your thought life positive. Visualize God shaping you to His design. (Philippians 4:8)
- Be open to wise counsel from others. Proverbs 11:14

QUESTIONS TO PONDER:

- Is it wrong for a believer to be depressed? Why or why not?
- Does time lessen or increase the emotions that result from painful experiences?
- What is the difference between happiness and joy?
- Read Romans 8:37-39. How do these verses give us an answer to depression?

UNDERSTANDING GRIEF

Unfortunately, if we live long enough, we will all experience grief. Many churches have classes available to assist its members through this unavoidable experience. The stages of grief are discussed in many books and are helpful if a class is not available. Sometimes taking the first step to recovery is the most difficult. You may find that a friend may be a helpful, listening ear at times. By all means, take advantage of all these beneficial sources that are available to you. Others care about you and want to help.

Depression is one of the stages of grief. It is normal when following a loss or death. It's important that we experience all the normal stages of grief and that we take them at our own pace. Everyone handles a loss differently. We should understand, though, that there is a time to "move on" and "live in the now." This applies to other types of loss as well. Again, it's important to take action and ask for help. Help is available. Read God's Word regularly. The following promises will bring you comfort and direction.

CHOOSE TO LIVE IN THE NOW, AND REJOICE IN CHRIST ALWAYS
*PROMISES TO CLAIM EVERYDAY

When you need a Savior	Acts 16:31; Romans 10:9-10; 13
When you doubt your salvation	I John 5:13; John 5:24; John 10:27-29
When you are lonely	Deuteronomy 31:6-8; Proverbs 18:24
When you feel frustrated	Isaiah 26:3-4; Matthew 11:28-30 Ephesians 2:14; Romans 5:1
When you have sinned	I John 1:9; Proverbs 28:13 Psalms 86:5; Psalms 103:12
When you need direction	James 1:5; Proverbs 2:8; Proverbs 3:5-6
When you are tempted to complain	Philippians 1:6; 2:13-14; Psalms 118:24, 29
When you are afraid	Psalms 27:1, 14; 56:3; Isaiah 41:10; 2 Timothy 1:7
When you experience sorrow	Lamentations 3:22-23
When you have trials	I Corinthians 10:13; Philippians 4:13; Galatians 2:20
When you are in need	Philippians 4:19; Matthew 6:33
When you are worried	Philippians 4:6-8; I Peter 5:7

For we are God's Masterpiece. He has created us anew in Christ Jesus, so that we can do the good things He planned for us long ago.
Ephesians 2:10 (NLT)

3. God's Masterpiece

You're Not By Chance

You are a masterpiece! Your DNA is unique to you. Your fingerprint is unique. You were designed by the Master Designer of this universe, the One who hung the stars in space, for one purpose – to glorify Him! Your parents, family heritage, national origin, were all designed just for you. God has a plan for your life.

Read Psalm 139:14-16

What does this passage mean to you?

AN OVERVIEW OF TEMPERAMENTS

Many authors and counselors divide personalities into four primary groups. These temperaments can be labeled in various ways with many secondary combinations of these four. A popular way of naming the temperaments is: Choleric, Sanguine, Melancholy, and Phlegmatic.

The first two are considered extroverts whereas the last two are more introverted. If we were to assign a specific task to a group, we would find that the pure temperaments within the group would probably respond in these ways:

>Cholerics: complete a task "My Way."
>
>Sanguines: complete a task the "Fun Way."
>
>Melancholies: complete a task the "Right Way."
>
>Phlegmatics: complete a task the "Easy Way."

Whereas this may be considered an oversimplification, it does help us discern where our overall strengths and weaknesses are. If we have an understanding of the way other people see us, we can better work and interact together. Since opposites attract, often married couples are of opposite temperaments. If we don't recognize this, it can present communication challenges in everyday life experiences. The way we approach and resolve problems may be different.

Understanding the temperaments of children helps us to know how to encourage their strengths and how to help them overcome their weaknesses. Showing appreciation for the strengths of a spouse and focusing on their positive qualities help to maintain harmony in a marriage. Focusing on weaknesses may be destructive to the relationship.

3. God's Masterpiece

The **Choleric** is a great leader and often takes charge when given the opportunity. He or she has a strong will and aspires to accomplish what they start. (I will continue only with "he" from this point on, but please realize both genders can fit all four categories equally.) He is confident, therefore not easily discouraged. He is often organized and very goal oriented. He looks for practical solutions to problems. He has little need for friends and is often a workaholic. He loves to be in control.

The **Sanguine** is the "Life of the Party." He has a great sense of humor. He is emotional and animated. He makes friends easily. He is great on stage, wide-eyed, and innocent. He has a changeable disposition, loves spontaneity, and is always a child at heart. He is quick to volunteer and he inspires others to join. He apologizes quickly and doesn't hold grudges. He has energy and enthusiasm for tasks and thrives on compliments. He is envied by others.

The **Melancholy** appreciates beauty and is sensitive to others. He is talented and creative, often musical or artistic. He is analytical, thinks deeply and is serious and purposeful. He is often self-sacrificing and prone to be a perfectionist. He is scheduled and detail oriented. He is able to see the main problem and will find creative solutions. He likes charts, figures, lists, etc. He makes friends cautiously and is content to stay in the background. He is faithful and devoted.

The **Phlegmatic** has a low-key personality, easy-going, and relaxed. He hides his emotions and is agreeable. He is calm, cool and collected, quiet and witty. He is patient and well balanced. He has administrative ability but likes to avoid conflict. He is a good listener and has a dry sense of humor. He has many friends and enjoys watching people. He is good under pressure but looks for the easy way to resolve problems.

WEAKNESSES OF THE TEMPERAMENTS

Choleric: Bossy, impatient, inflexible, doesn't compliment others, argumentative, rude, manipulative, uses and dominates others, stubborn, refuses to apologize.

Sanguine: Compulsive talker, exaggerates, loud, egotistical, complains, forgets obligations, undisciplined, controlled by feelings, makes excuses, and interrupts.

Melancholy: Remembers negatives, moody, self-centered, introspective, low self-image, hard to please, deep need for approval, critical of others, unforgiving.

Phlegmatic: Unenthusiastic, indecisive, irresponsible, selfish, lazy, would rather watch than participate, dampens enthusiasm, stays uninvolved, judges others, resists change.

The most important point to understand in this brief study of temperaments is that we are all uniquely designed by the Creator of the universe. We are all a blend of these temperaments and we all have God given strengths. We also have weaknesses that we should be aware of and be willing to turn over to God's control for Him to correct.

We will never reach perfection in this life. However as we turn our mind, will and emotions over to Him, He will bring us to be more like Christ each day.

Review Romans 8:29-30 and write God's ultimate purpose for you:

The temperament of Jesus is perfectly balanced. Our desire should be to be more like Him each day. The more we submit to His Lordship, the more Christ-like we will be.

Remember! "No one can be 'like Jesus' better than Jesus can!"

How would you describe your personality or temperament?

What are your strengths?
What are your weaknesses?
What does God want to do in us according to Ezekiel 36:25-27?

YOU are a masterpiece, one of a kind, created by the one and only God of the universe. The One who spoke and light flooded the darkness! The One who put every star in place! So, look up into the sky on a clear night and thank the One who put all the stars there for loving you and creating you the way you are!

Remember! You are still a work in progress! He's not finished with you yet!

Look up Ephesians 2:10. (Write it in your journal)

If anyone considers himself religious and yet does not keep a tight rein on his tongue, he deceives himself and his religion is worthless.
James 1:26 (NIV)

4. What Did You Say?

Tongue Control

The first sound we made when we entered this world was probably an unhappy, uncontrolled cry! Our tongue was working great! As a newborn, we just went through an extremely uncomfortable process that took us from a safe, secure zone, to a new environment that we perceived as not nearly as peaceful. Bright lights, loud voices and cold air became our new experience! Our tongue and our lungs kicked into gear as we reacted!

As we grow we learn to make interesting sounds and begin the process of learning to communicate with this new world around us. We learn while we are young the power that we have when we use our voice. We discover that at 2:00 am we can bring attention to our needs easily by communicating to our caregivers, who are sound asleep, that we need them to come to our aid!

We also learn at a young age that what we say has consequences. The Bible speaks clearly of the responsibility that we, as believers, have to manage and control what comes out of our mouth. Words have meaning! Once they are spoken they cannot be retracted.

Our Creator is truly amazing! The more we understand the body, the more we realize we don't know! The physical construction of the tongue, nose, mouth, and vocal chords is highly technical and an interesting study. The author has studied it somewhat as a vocalist in college. When taking voice lessons you learn to control the body parts that change your voice tone. Our voice works closely with the ears and air supply as we control volume and pitch, as well as tone.

A TOPICAL BIBLE STUDY

By now you should have enough of an understanding of the Bible to enable you to do a topical study. This may be a small stretch for you, but if you were teaching a Bible study on the topic of "the tongue," what discussion questions would stimulate responses from those in your class?

Start a new section in your notebook for "Bible Studies". As you organize the studies that you write you may want to begin with a list of Scriptures on a specific topic. For this one, look up verses in the concordance that use the word "tongue" and also "words", "speak", "mouth", etc.

Doing a Word Study is not difficult but it requires some time. As we search the Scriptures we hope to accomplish two objectives:

- As we study about the tongue, and similar words relating to it, we will make an unpleasant topic more "palatable". Realize that even though this is a serious topic it can also be taken somewhat lightly. Don't expect it to be on the level of a Master of Divinity's writing. No one will be scrutinizing your work.
- As you attempt to organize your thoughts and Scriptures you will, in fact, begin to learn how to do a word study. By learning this you open the door, ever so slightly, to the possibility that God might be able to use you to guide or teach someone else.

When we do a topical study it's to glean truths from God's Word on a particular subject. The purpose of a topical study is to organize and apply Scripture on the topic, for your own edification or spiritual growth, and for the purpose of teaching others.

Steps to follow in doing a topical study:
1. Find a good concordance.
2. Begin by looking up as many verses as you can find on the subject of the tongue and other related words. (List benefits from a God controlled tongue. See Proverbs 12:18)
3. Take notes on each verse. Categorize them as you go.
4. List verses that refer to a controlled tongue and those that refer to an uncontrolled tongue (For example, lying, slander, lips. See Proverbs 12:17-19; 13:2-3)
5. List comparisons to the tongue. (Ex. James 3:6)
6. Arrange the verses into an outline.

7. List some passages that show results of both positive and negative words.

8. Expand the outline by using life experiences or illustrations to help make the application.

FOR FURTHER STUDY CONSIDER THE FOLLOWING:

 *Read Genesis 1:3.*

Write the words that God spoke. What happened as a result?

1. Think about the power that was displayed by God's words. How have God's Words changed you?
2. What promise does the Psalmist give us in Psalm 34:12-13?
3. What does it mean to bless another person?
4. Give an example of words that are used to bless and to curse:
5. What is slander?
6. What part do anger and jealousy play in slander? (Be sure to emphasize what the Bible says!)

 *Read 2 Timothy 2:23-24.*

What do these verses say that we should we avoid?

Now, consider what you've learned and meditate (think and pray) on it.

- Ask God to give you insights into what you have learned.

4. What Did You Say?

- Ask Him to show you if you have a weakness in the area of the tongue.
- Personal applications should always result in personal spiritual enrichment.
- Summarize what you have learned from your topical study on "the tongue."

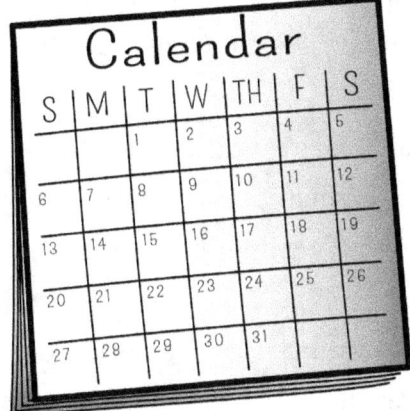

Commit to the Lord whatever you do and your plans will succeed.
Proverbs 16:3 (NIV)

5. Redeeming My Time

The Balancing Act

"I just don't have time," "I'm too busy"! How often do we say things like this? Yet, all of us have the same amount of time, usually 8,760 hours a year, unless it's a leap year. What we do with our time is the key.

"Teach us to number our days aright, that we may gain a heart of wisdom." (Psalm 90:12, NIV) The New Testament says "Redeem the time" or "Make the most of every opportunity." We can't manage our life unless we manage our time.

Many books have been written on time management and priorities. One of the most famous is "The Purpose Driven Life" by Rick Warren.

It helps us not only to define our purpose but to prioritize what we do. If you have not read this book it is highly recommended. Once we have determined our purpose then it is much easier to eliminate certain responsibilities.

Today's family is often pulled in many different directions. This causes undo stress. The important is often at the mercy of the urgent. The book "The Tyranny of the Urgent" reminds us of this. Mary and Martha illustrate this in the Bible.

A generation or two ago, life was much less complicated. Most men worked and most women were home and cared for the needs of the family. Today many husbands travel or commute long hours and hardly spend any time with their family because of what their job demands. Their "Super Mom" wife also works, sometimes with equally long hours, and cares for the family too.

Many of us pay the price in broken or strained relationships, neglected children, unhealthy eating habits, poorly planned meals, and resulting weight and health problems.

Before we can begin to balance our time we need to define our purpose. Our life's purpose should live on after we are gone. Proverbs 19:21 (NIV) says "Many are the plans in a man's heart, but it is the Lord's purpose that prevails." Ask God what His purpose is for your life. It may take some time to hear His voice. Be concise. Write it in one sentence.

 *My primary purpose is:*

5. Redeeming My Time

Now, let's look at a typical week in your life. Think about your family, your work schedule and other demands. Write down at least ten things that occupy your time in order of priority.

My priorities are: (Record in your notebook beside each one the time spent for 7 full days. Remember to take into account your drive time.) Think about how they relate to your primary purpose.

1) _____ _____hours

2) _____ _____hours

3) _____ _____hours

4) _____ _____hours

5) _____ _____hours

6) _____ _____hours

7) _____ _____hours

8) _____ _____hours

9) _____ _____hours

10) _____ _____hours

                                             TOTAL _____ hours

Other commitments in addition to the above: Additional total hours: _____

What is your total time commitment for the week? How much time is left over? (Subtract total hours from 168, the total hours in a week.) _____hours.

You may have heard the phrase "you spell love T-I-M-E." That is so true. Does what you spend your time on accurately illustrate your priorities? Why or why not?

What activities do you need to eliminate from your schedule?

What other changes do you need to make in your schedule in order to give your priorities more time?

For those who desire it, many direct sales companies, as well as traditional companies, offer opportunities to work from the home. Some have sizeable income opportunities. Are you willing to do whatever God leads you to do in order to reduce your stress and keep your priorities in line?

COMMON SENSE WAYS TO REDUCE STRESS AND MANAGE TIME:

- Make a list of what you need to do each day. Put the most important first, then the most difficult next.
- Complete each task that you start before you start another one.
- Enlist help when possible. Galatians 6:2 (NIV) says "Carry each other's burdens, and in this way you will fulfill the law of Christ."
- Focus on the job at hand and avoid interruptions. Let your voice mail answer the phone. Remember there are very few emergencies. If you do answer, you may need to learn to say, "I can talk 5 minutes now, or I can call you back later. Which is better for you?"
- Make every trip count. Combine all errands into one trip if possible.
- Learn to fix healthy but simple meals. Avoid mixes and canned soups that have unhealthy additives. Use fresh vegetables and fruits instead of processed. Stir-fried foods in olive oil are healthy and fast. If you are "health conscious," limit soft drinks,

salt, sugar, caffeine, and white flour in your daily diet. This can boost energy!
- Ladies, keep a simple hairstyle. One that doesn't require a lot of maintenance.
- Again, ladies, organize your closet. As much as possible wear solid colors that "mix and match," with year-round fabrics that are easy care.
- Get plenty of rest. Go to bed at the same time every night. Avoid computer games or computer work after 8pm. Most people require at least 7 or 8 hours of sleep every night.
- Avoid eating after 8 p.m.
- Take a multiple vitamin and additional B complex vitamins when you are stressed.

Illness can bring additional stress to a family. Sometimes it takes many hours out of our normally busy schedule to care for family members or to take the time to recover from illness ourselves. Eating healthy, exercising, and getting adequate rest go a long way to staying healthy.

Regular medical check-ups are important to be sure that health is maintained. Hormone imbalance is sometimes the cause of physical symptoms. Imbalance in the endocrine glands are sometimes a challenge to diagnose correctly. There is much that doctors can do to help us when we are sick, but a healthy lifestyle is our responsibility.

Do I need to lose weight and improve my eating habits?

How can I be more of a blessing to my spouse?

How can I as a Christian be a blessing to my family? Read Proverbs 20:7; 22:6

Read Psalm 126:3-5. How are our children a blessing to us?

What attributes and character traits am I responsible for instilling in my children?

Read Deuteronomy 4:9; 11:19-21

What specifically do I need to do to teach my children (and grandchildren) to love God and desire to obey Him?

Read Acts 16:1 and 2 Timothy 1:5

What do these verses show us about the importance of passing our faith on to the next generations?

For our struggle is not against flesh and blood, but against the rulers against the authorities, against the powers of this dark world and against the spiritual forces of evil in the heavenly realms. Ephesians 6:12 (NIV)

6. Struggles Within

Understanding Submission

All law comes from God's Law as given to us in the Bible. Society and governments are built on the pillars of submission and the authority that is given them by God. Without authority, laws could not be enforced. There would be chaos everywhere.

The thirteenth chapter of Romans discusses the origin and importance of government and authority. Each of us, no matter who we are, has authority figures in our lives. No one, not even the President, should ignore the law. There are local, state, and federal laws that we are to obey. Every time we drive a car we have to obey traffic lights, stop signs, and speed limits.

At work, we often have policies that we must adhere to in order to keep our job and to keep order in the workplace. Children learn at a very young age that there are consequences when they don't obey the rules at home and at school. This is true throughout life.

So, submission to authority in society should become a way of life. Unfortunately, we have seen a weakening of authority and an increase of rebellion in our society over the past generation. God has made it clear what we can expect to happen when we fail to obey the authorities in our life.

Summarize Romans 13 and write phrases related to submission in your notebook. Also note the reference.

Read and paraphrase what these Scriptures say in your notebook.

    I Peter 2:13-25

    James 4:7

    Ephesians 5:21-30

    Hebrews 12:5-11

    Hebrews 13:15-17

    Colossians 3:12-25

The most important factor in submission is the attitude of the heart. Love is the motivation that makes submission a blessing. Obedience to authority keeps our conscience clear and keeps our joy alive. That's how we win when we submit. Power struggles can cause strain in any relationship and "score" may sometimes be kept to see who wins in a certain situation.

6. STRUGGLES WITHIN

The Bible promises blessings to those who obey their authorities and submit one to another. When we give the other person's choices and desires a preference over ours, we are the true winners.

Read the following verses and write the promise God gives:

Deuteronomy 6:1-9
Ephesians 6:1-3
Hebrews 11:8-12

In a family unit there may be a struggle for power. Just as in a government, a business, a church, an organization, there must be a "head" in the family. Without leadership, the family unit doesn't function properly. The Bible asks the husband to be the leader and the wife and children to follow his lead. Each person is equal before God, and should never be considered less valuable or less important than the other.

Submitting to a husband and father who loves his family as Christ loves the Church is easy. When an authority is selfish and self-serving, it becomes more difficult. No one should remain under any authority who is abusive and demeaning or tries to influence us to disobey God.

Even though we are not studying about abusive relationships, if you are in one, help is available. You do not deserve the abuse. The percentage of women within the average church who are being or have been abused is staggering. So, realize, you are not alone. If you don't know who to talk to, let your group leader or pastor know privately so they can assist you. Get help NOW!

READ EPHESIANS 5:22-6:4.

Summarize what you learn.

In the Bible we find three words translated as our one word "love." Look up the meaning of each in a Bible Dictionary.

1) EROS
2) PHILEO (Philia)
3) AGAPE

Which of these loves is expressed in the following references?

1) Ruth 1:16-18
2) Judges 14:1-3
3) I John 3:16

Which type of love can only be expressed in a Christian marriage? Why?

Below are some expressions of love that we all need. Comment on why each one is important.

Acceptance
Understanding
Loyalty
Communication

In an earlier chapter we discussed God's love. How has He expressed His love to you?

How can you express your love to Him?

In what ways do you need to show your love more to your family?

JEALOUSY

Jealousy is normally a struggle for power or control. We can read of the first rebellion, a result of Satan's jealousy, in the Bible. There are many unanswered questions about the fall of Lucifer (Satan). There's not a lot in the Bible about it. Apparently Satan was jealous of God and chose to rebel against Him. Pride and rebellion are opposites of submission and obedience and are the root cause of most conflicts.

When Jesus was tempted in the desert we see the true motivations of our enemy. He desires power and control. He wants to be worshipped. Because of the sin of Adam, which followed the fall of Lucifer, mankind continues to battle the forces of darkness.

Jealousy, pride, and rebellion still raise their ugly heads. We are all tempted to give in to the desires of the flesh. We should pray and "reckon" our pride dead. (See Galatians 2:20) and ask God for an obedient heart. Remember? The attitude of Christ is that of a servant.

 *Read and write the following: Philippians 2:5-8*

When we surrender our pride and selfishness, we find joy in serving others instead of desiring to be served. We receive power to resist the enemy.

Read Matthew 4:1-11.

What did the Devil tempt Jesus to do?

What is the significance of each one?

The struggle between good and evil will continue until God brings it to a close at the End of Time. Until then, we are part of the struggle. God's Spirit is drawing us to Himself and the enemy is trying to defeat us. For this reason we should daily put on the armor of God (Ephesians 6:11) and resist the enemy in the power of God.

Any time we disobey God we leave an opportunity for the devil to get a stronghold in our life. Our testimony may be harmed and our joy will suffer. Even though our eternity with Christ is secure in Him because of what Christ did for us on the Cross, we can experience defeat in our daily walk if we choose to disobey.

Obedience should be our goal. Following Christ daily is our privilege. Jesus asked us to take up our cross and follow Him.

Read Luke 9:23.

What does this Scripture mean to you?

He (the godly) is like a tree planted by streams of water, which yields its fruit in season and whose leaf does not wither. Whatever he does prospers.
Psalm 1:1 (NIV)

7. Pursuing Godliness

"As the deer pants for streams of water, so my soul pants for you, O God. My soul thirsts for God, for the living God. Where can I go and meet with God?" (Psalm 42:1-2 NIV) Desiring to meet with God is evidence of a godly life. Remember our study on hearing God's voice? Obeying the voice of God is important each day. As we grow in Christ we will be able to discern more and more of His will for us. His still small voice and nudge becomes precious.

We learn discernment. We learn when God is speaking. Sometimes it's okay to say "no" to people. Not everything that well-meaning people ask of us is God's will for us. Obeying God doesn't mean that we become a doormat for everyone who wants to use us or take advantage of us. (For example, we shouldn't be pressured to work overtime without pay. Neither should we feel obligated to fill a position in the church just because there is a need.)

However, when we know that God wants us to do something, we should obey cheerfully! It's there that we find true joy! The ultimate purpose of a godly life is to bring glory to God by being totally surrendered to Him. Because God has given us all unique personalities, there is variety in the way He expresses Himself through us.

Meditate on the following verse: **Ephesians 4:13** in the Berkley translation says:

"Until we all may arrive at the unity of faith and that understanding of the Son of God that brings completeness of personality, tending toward the measure of the stature of the fullness of Christ."

The qualities that are seen in a godly man or woman encompass what he or she looks like, what we are, what we say, and how we live.

 *What did you learn about godliness?*

We're going to get a little personal here as we make the application of godliness to each of us.

The following section is to be answered by women only. The men's section will follow.

A. A GODLY WOMAN (Women only answer)

How would you describe "inner beauty" or "spiritual sparkle"?

1. What do each of the following verses say is the source for inner beauty?
   John 15:5
   2 Corinthians 3:18
   John 3:30
   2 Peter 1:4
   Titus 2:3
   Acts 6:15
   Proverbs 31:26
   I Corinthians 13:4-5

2. What is a meek and quiet spirit? (See 1 Peter 3:4)
3. What is your definition of poise?
4. Which Scriptures from above illustrate poise?
5. Why is our appearance important?
6. Man looks on our outward appearance. (I Samuel 16:7) What does God look upon?
7. Can the principle in I Corinthians 9:22-23 apply to our appearance? Why or why not?
8. How does our outward appearance effect unbelievers?

B. A GODLY MAN (Men only answer)

As you consider the following questions, listen to the nudging of God's Spirit. Godly men are the hope of this nation, and our families. Becoming a spiritual giant is possible when you seek God's will for your life daily. We need faithful men to stand up for biblical values and lead our nation back to God.

A godly man possesses the following qualities:

(List these qualities in your notebook and circle the ones that describe you.)

gentle	generous	confident	integrity
honest	patient	not lazy	submissive
faithful	disciplined	loving	resourceful

1. What should the spiritual role of a man be in the home?
2. What is the husband's role in the discipline of children?
3. How should a husband love his wife according to Ephesians 5:25?
4. What should a man's role be in the church?
5. Should men be actively involved in the community? If so, how?
6. Why are a man's habits important?
7. Who looks on our outward appearance? (I Samuel 16:7) What does God look upon?

8. What is the significance of the principle in I Corinthians 9:22-23 to our appearance?

9. How does our outward appearance affect unbelievers according to John 17:15-19?

C. TO BE ANSWERED BY BOTH MEN AND WOMEN:

A godly person reflects Christ.

1. What should be the motive of our heart in regard to the way we look, especially the way we dress? (See 1 Corinthians 10:31)

2. What is integrity? (See Psalm 25:21)

3. Does our appearance suggest that we have integrity and honesty? Why or why not?

4. Why is integrity important in the following verses?
   Psalm 139:23-24
   Job 2:3
   Proverbs 17:9
   Matthew 5:23-24
   Proverbs 31:11

5. What is the Biblical principle taught in Hosea 7:8-9 and Psalm 106:35?

6. Paraphrase the following:
   1 Corinthians 3:16
   1 Corinthians 6:19
   2 Corinthians 6:16

7. What is the significance of our body being called the temple of God?

8. Why did Paul use this term in reference to us?

9. What should you do in order to take better care of God's temple?

Write Philippians 1:6 in your journal:

How would you rate yourself on the following qualities? (From 1-5 with 5 being good)

dependability	punctuality
gratefulness	truthfulness
forgiveness	generosity
discipline	obedience to God
balance	humility
diligence	submission

God has promised to complete the work that He has started in us. Just like the Master Potter, God is molding and making our lives into a beautiful vessel. When we submit to His hands, as the clay submits to the hands of the Potter, our life is transformed!

Isaiah 64:8 *says: "We are the clay, you are the potter."*

How is the perspective of the potter different from that of the clay?

 *Write Ephesians 2:10 in your journal.*

YOU are a unique workmanship of God. You can be YOU and still be a godly man or woman, full of God's Grace. As you have already seen, you don't have to be perfect. You can be yourself and be totally accepted because of WHOSE you are.

Our confidence as individuals comes from KNOWING Christ, ALLOWING His Spirit to fill us, and RESTING in who we are in Him.

THOUGHTS TO PONDER:

God loves us just the way we are - but He loves us too much to leave us where we are!

What godly characteristics need to be developed in your life?

*Therefore go and make disciples of all nations, baptizing them in the name of the Father and of the Son and of the Holy Spirit, and teaching them to obey everything I have commanded you. And surely I am with you always, to the very end of the age.
Matthew 28:19-20 (NIV)*

8. Pass It On

"It Only Takes a Spark"

A popular song a few decades ago was called "Pass it On." The first words to the song were "It only takes a spark." The message of the song was about the influence that one person can have to see God begin to change a home, a church, and a nation. Your testimony is special! Your path that God brings you along is unique. You HAVE a message to share! You CAN make a difference! You may be one that God uses to impact the world!

How BLESSED we are to be God's child! His glorious riches are ours in Christ Jesus! Take a few minutes to review some of these truths with me from Unit I.

DECLARE THESE TRUTHS FROM SCRIPTURE:

- I am born again by the blood of the Lamb. (Romans 5:9; Ephesians 1:7)
- My sins are washed away in the blood of the Lamb. (John 1:29)
- I am in the Lamb of God who takes away the sin of the world. (Ephesians 1:4)
- I am born again by the incorruptible Word of God that lives and abides forever. (1 Peter 1:23).
- I am a new creation in Christ Jesus, old things are passed away, all things are become new, (2 Corinthians 5:17)
- I was chosen in Christ Jesus before the foundation of the world. (Ephesians 1:4)
- I am accepted in the Beloved. (Ephesians 1:4-6)
- I am sealed with the Holy Spirit unto the day of Redemption. (Ephesians 1:13)
- I am reconciled to God, through the blood of the Cross. (Romans 5:10)
- I am justified, declared righteous in Christ Jesus. (Romans 5:1,9)
- I have been crucified with Christ. (Gal. 2:20; Romans 6:4,11)
- I have been resurrected with Christ. (Gal. 2:20; Romans 6:4,11)
- I am seated with Christ in heavenly places. (Ephesians 1:3)
- Christ, who is above all demonic principalities and powers, lives in me. (Ephesians 1:21)
- I am more than a conqueror through Christ who loves me. (Romans 6:14,22; 8:37)
- I have the mind of Christ. (I Corinthians 2:16)
- I am the bride of Christ. (Revelation 22:17)
- I am the holy temple of God. Christ lives in me. (Colossians 1:27)

- I am an heir of God and a joint heir with Jesus Christ. (Ephesians 2:11; Romans 8:17)
- My citizenship is in Heaven. My name is written in the Lamb's Book of Life. (Ephesians 2:6)
- Nothing can separate me from the love of Christ Jesus my Lord. (Romans 8:38-39)
- I am God's purchased possession, bought by the blood of the Lamb. Sealed by the Holy Spirit. (Ephesians 1:13-14)
- I am God the Father's love gift to His Son. (Ephesians 1:14)
- God is my Father (Romans 8:15)
- Jesus is my Savior (Hebrews 9:28; Ephesians 2:8-9); Jesus is my Lord (John 11:27); Jesus is my intercessor (Hebrews 12:24); Jesus is my advocate (Hebrews 12:14-15); Jesus is my great High Priest (Hebrews 10:12; 9:11); Jesus is my Great Shepherd (Psalm. 23; Isaiah. 40:11); Jesus is my Coming King (Hebrews 9:28).

How blessed we are to KNOW the Creator of this vast universe in a personal way. What a privilege it is to share our faith with others. Witnessing should be an overflow from our own abundant life in Christ.

Witnessing is sharing our firsthand experience or testimony in the power of God's Spirit. When we are a witness in a court of law we are asked to tell what we personally know. We should just simply share God's Grace that is ours because of the life, death, burial, and resurrection of the Lord Jesus Christ. It's all about HIM!!

Often we allow fear of what others will think of us to keep us from sharing our faith. (This is a form of pride.) Our enemy, the Devil, often blinds us to the fact that witnessing isn't difficult and it's not about **us**.

So, what do we need to say and do when we share the Good News of Christ with someone? First, listen closely to what the person says. Determine if they are ready to hear the Gospel.

Write down these questions in your notebook and memorize them so you can diagnose where a person is in their search to know God.

- "Where do you attend church or what is your church background?" (Realize that many people attend church regularly but they don't have a relationship with Christ.)
- "If you died today do you know if you would go to Heaven?"
- "What do you think are the entrance requirements to Heaven?" (Listen for answers that imply they are trusting in something THEY can do to earn Heaven. This is evidence they don't understand why Christ died. Their answer should be about HIM not THEM!)
- Share your testimony of how you came to KNOW that you have eternal life in Christ.

Remember to include them in your notebook. Memorize the following Scriptures if possible so you can easily share them at any time you are given the opportunity.

8. Pass It On

A. We are all sinners and we can't go to Heaven on our own. (Write Romans 3:23)
B. God loves us and He wants us to know Him. He sent His Son to make that possible.
Write John 1:1; and 14
Write John 3:16
Our sin debt was paid when Christ died on the cross.
Write Romans 5:8
Write Romans 6:6
C. When we trust His death on the cross as payment for our sins and receive the forgiveness that He offers, we receive the gift of eternal life.
Write Ephesians 2:8-9
Write John 6:47

Ask them if they would like to receive forgiveness for their sins and the gift of Heaven when they die?

If they say "yes," lead them in a prayer of repentance similar to the following: "Lord Jesus, I know that I'm a sinner and that I cannot go to Heaven on my own. I realize for the first time that You came to Earth and died for my sin on the cross. I understand that You paid my sin debt in full. Thank You for dying in my place. Come into my life and be my Savior and Lord. Help me live for you every day. Amen."

 *Pray for them that they will begin to understand God's Word.*

 *Invite them to church and give them a copy of the Bible and this Bible study.*

 *Explain the importance of baptism.*

Explain that it identifies us with Christ symbolically just as a wedding ring identifies us with our spouse. It also pictures His death, burial, and resurrection. Encourage them to be baptized as their first act of obedience.

When you lead someone to a saving knowledge of Christ you will find it spiritually exhilarating! There is no other feeling like it! It's such a privilege to be a part in the spiritual "birthing" of another human being. It's thrilling to know someone will be in Heaven throughout eternity because you were willing to share God's love and grace with them! God could have chosen another method to share His Good News but he allows us to be blessed through sharing!

8. Pass It On

 *The Great Commission in Matthew 28:19-20 makes our privilege and our responsibility clear. Write and memorize these verses.*

What your Heaven will be like is being determined now by your obedient life on Earth. Imagine how your eternity will reflect your obedience to the Great Commission. As God opens the door of opportunity to share the Gospel we must be prepared, wherever we are. It may be at work, at a neighbor's, or when we're with a family member, or at the salon or doctor's office.

Most churches have lists of people who have visited the services and should have follow-up. You may want to ask your church leaders if they would like for you to visit some prospective members. If so, go with one or two others, trusting that God will lead you to those who need to know Him. If your church has an evangelism class, such as F.A.I.T.H. or Evangelism Explosion, consider being a part.

God's riches are ours throughout eternity but they are to be shared. Where would we be if someone had not shared with you and me?

So, can you answer the question "Who am I in Christ"? Will you share this message with others and leave the results to God?

Leader Helps
Unit 2

Chapter 1: Practicing Forgiveness

More than likely you have taken a break between the two units of study. It's helpful if each person has some extra time to do this first lesson because it can be overwhelming when we start to bring up the past hurts that we've experienced. If you are able, encourage each person in the class to look over this lesson about a month before you plan to start back. If someone has been physically or emotionally hurt in the past there needs to be time for them to begin to deal with it as a new believer and get the counseling they may need.

When you meet together everyone should be ready to start the lesson that day. Before you begin, spend some time sharing what has happened during the break with each class member and ask a few people in advance to share how they have grown as a believer.

Before you close, if possible, have someone give a testimony (it might need to be you) of how being able to forgive someone has impacted their life. Unbelievers can't understand forgiveness in the way we as believers can. God's grace enables us to forgive. We can't do it in our own strength. Remind them of how Christ suffered for us, yet He forgave those who betrayed him as well as all of us whose sin He paid for on the cross.

Close with prayer.

Chapter 2: Emotions in Motion

As a leader it may be a challenge to relate this lesson to everyone in the class. None of us are the same when it comes to this topic. God has "wired" us all so differently. Don't expect everyone to respond to the subject in the same way.

In general, as we mature as believers our emotions become more controlled by the Holy Spirit. As we grow in Christlikeness we will exhibit more of the Fruit of the Spirit. (Review those from Galatians 5.)

In this study we don't discuss the enemy a lot. He was defeated at the cross and because of the resurrection of Christ he has no authority over us as children of God. He does still attack us as believers when we allow sin to get a stronghold in our life and our emotions are where we are often targeted.

Some ways that the enemy attacks us:
- Fear – the enemy is able to use other people's words and actions to cause doubt and concern and fear. (Read 2 Timothy 1:7.)
- Anger – the enemy also uses this emotion which basically is frustration over not getting our way or having control. (James 1:19-20)
- Jealousy – the enemy uses this to appeal to our fleshly desires. It usually involves a person but it can carry over into possessions as well.

- Disappointment (Depression) – the enemy attacks us by accusing God in our minds of not caring for us and giving us what we want or what we think we need.

Our mind is the battleground for spiritual warfare. If the enemy can control our thought life then he gains a stronghold in our life. That's why guarding what we look at, listen to, and speak is so important!

Emotions overall are good. We would be like robots without them. They enable us to enjoy life and have fun! They bring humor into our world! Though, when a believer is emotionally unstable before they trust Christ they may need counseling and guidance in their relationships for a time.

Discuss the comparison of Hannah, and the Virtuous Woman.
- Both women were of noble character
- Their husbands trusted their judgment
- They were respected in the community
- They spoke words of wisdom
- They watched over their households.

What does the disappointment of David teach us?
- God doesn't always give us the desires of our heart
- God wants to teach us of His Sufficiency
- God wants to take us deeper in our faith

In closing, review the list of how to "Experience Victory over Depression."

Remind them that we as believers must actively apply God's Word in order to have victory over depression. We must read God's Word and rest in His power to bring us through difficult times.

Close in prayer for those who are struggling with their emotions.

Chapter 3: "God's Masterpiece"

This is a fun lesson and will give a little break from the intense lesson we had last time. During the study time each person probably has figured out the different types of personalities that live in their household and maybe those people they work with.

There are several personality tests online and many different approaches that people take in determining the types of personalities. (If you google the word "temperament" you will see what I mean.) By no means is this supposed to be taken too seriously. It is more helpful if we try at first to only apply what we are studying to oneself. The reason it has been included is to help us recognize our uniqueness and to help us cooperate with God as He is working on our weaknesses.

No where do we find this taught in the Bible in this way. So, enjoy the break this week. Suggest that each person, if they want to study this further, check out books by Tim and Beverly LaHaye on the subject. (ie: "Spirit Controlled Temperament")

Chapter 4: What Did You Say?

When you saw the subject of this lesson the first time you may have panicked! The purpose of this lesson is to cover what we "say" that sometimes causes offense to others. We also include the subject of speaking blessings on others as well. Since in certain contexts this subject can be controversial we suggest you limit it to what is in the lesson. (At a later time we may go into more detail in the context of Spiritual gifts.)

You may want to suggest that they include a study of the word "Word" and "Mouth" along with "Tongue" to give them more Scriptures to study. Consider the entire Bible as a source for this lesson because it is wholly God's Word, revealed to us.

Some questions that might lead to discussion are:
- Have you ever said something that you regret?
- Have you ever made a vow? Have you kept it?
- Is it possible to have a God-controlled mouth?
- Have you ever spoken an untruth (ie: lied?)
- What should be our motivation when we speak?

Learning to control our tongue, to think and pray before we speak is a discipline that takes time. The benefits of "tongue control" is amazing. Negative thinking produces negative speaking. Therefore as we mature as believers we will more and more speak positive, edifying words.

The second purpose for the lesson is to provide motivation for each person to begin learning how to compile Scriptures together and do a "word study" on their own. As we grow as believers God may open opportunities to teach a class or speak to a group. This is a beginning for those in the class to learn to listen to God as He leads them in this way. Don't be surprised if someone in the group shows spiritual giftedness in this area. You may have a new preacher or evangelist in your group!!

ant
Chapter 5: Redeeming My Time

The class time for this lesson may be brief because most of the lesson is personal and not necessarily to be shared within the group. It can be life altering though if it causes the group to seriously consider some changes in their life. Some people may quit their job and others may decide to begin considering a new direction in their life if they start prioritizing their time more and begin listening to God with an open heart.

You might consider taking a class break this week and resume with the next lesson.

Chapter 6: Struggles Within

This lesson can be quite timely on the heels of last week's lesson. The ramifications of this chapter could potentially cause some to make additional changes in their family as they determine to follow the biblical principles that they are studying.

Some women may choose to limit the authority figures in their life to that of God, husband, pastor, and the government. (The writer has worked outside of the home very little for this reason.) Sometimes women are afraid to "think outside the box" and considered their options. They may have never thought about this subject from the biblical perspective. In some cases it may lead to making a change. There are many ways to contribute to the financial needs of the household without working in the corporate world.

Men, also, at times feel they must submit to a boss who is not following biblical principles and the boss's poor choices and misplaced priorities may carry over and affect them as an employee, causing undo stress in the family. The important thing is to listen to what God is leading you to do. When we follow godly principles we will be blessed.

Chapter 7: Pursuing Godliness

This chapter may be a challenge. It may take you out of your "comfort zone". Godliness is a topic that we don't hear about often. It includes giving God control of our whole being, body, soul, and spirit. It includes what you look like on the outside and the inside. It includes our habits, our dreams, our goals, our desires, all of our being, being conformed to God's will and to His likeness!

From a personal perspective I'd like to share a few things. I have been a public speaker for many years. (By no means a famous one.) However, I've spoken to thousands of women for over 30 years about who they are in Christ and how they should value themselves as creations of their Heavenly Father.

One thing I love to share with women is how to dress so that they are attractive but in a godly way. A lady should dress so that people notice her eyes and her countenance. So often women are ignorant of "eye traps" that draw attention to areas that aren't flattering or modest. Simply educating young women can make a huge difference in the way they are perceived in the workplace or at school, etc.

Because this is so close to my heart I had to include it in this study. If I can be of any additional help in this area please feel free to contact me.

Integrity someone has said means – doing the right thing when no one is looking. That is true, but is there ever really a time when no one is looking? No, because God is always with us. Our integrity is reflected in our appearance. As believers, we are all the temple of God, being conformed to His likeness.

Chapter 8: Pass It On

Witnessing is sharing Christ in the power of the Spirit and leaving the results to God. This last chapter simplifies witnessing so that the "fear factor" is eliminated. There is nothing complicated about sharing Christ. The first thing a believer needs to do is write, then memorize, a simple testimony about what God has done in their life since they came to know Him. (Some examples may be – they now have real purpose, their fear is gone, they have a new hope, etc.) Once they share it a few times then they can begin sharing a little more Scripture.

Remind each one that Christ is the one who will be leading them when they have prayed and asked Him to. He is faithful to lead us when we are willing to go!

Thank you for being willing to allow God to use you to touch the lives in the class. It is my prayer that you will be abundantly blessed because of your obedience and your faithfulness in teaching His Word.

There will be coming soon an additional study of Romans 6-8, entitled "Transformed - Into His Likeness" on the Spirit-filled life, by the same author.

Rejoicing in Him!
Jerri Mason

About the Author

Jerri Mason's life has centered round church and church music from a young age. She began accompanying a children's choir when she was ten. As a teen she felt God's call to ministry. She answered His call but didn't have clarity yet as to what He was calling her to do. She sensed that God had gifted her in the area of music and decided to pursue that as a profession.

As a young married adult, she felt His call again. She began to search the Scriptures wanting to know everything God had for her. In the early 1970s Reverend Cliff Palmer came to her church as the new pastor. Hearing entire books of the Bible explained precept upon precept increased her understanding. The deeper truths of the Scriptures came alive and she came to realize it was her blueprint for life. Jerri and her husband, Rick, along with many others, became involved in

Evangelism Explosion and the church bus ministry, reaching out to the Northwest Arkansas area.

In the 1980s she moved to Oklahoma where she served there on the staff of a church as director of childhood education. The church started backyard Bible clubs bringing many children to know Christ. Jerri looked for a new believer's book that could be used to help them establish habits of growth in God's Word. That was the beginning of the vision for this book.

In the 1990s Premier Designs, Inc. opened a door to ministry for Jerri outside the walls of the church. She saw God use this company to touch the lives of thousands around the world for Christ. Jerri has been privileged to stand before women, in small and large groups, and share with them that they are uniquely designed and valued by God.

The most recent move has been back to Northwest Arkansas. Her family has gone through challenging times while there. Yet, God is faithful. No matter what dagger the enemy continues to hurl at the family, she knows: "God's Word is Truth! Stand there! He will bring the victory!"

http://www.GraceIsMine.com
jerriandrick@gmail.com
https://www.facebook.com/jerrilynnmason

www.ingramcontent.com/pod-product-compliance
Lightning Source LLC
Chambersburg PA
CBHW050202130526
44591CB00034B/1783